LUMINOUS
HEART
OF THE
EARTH

Also by Robert and Rachel Olds

Luminous Heart of Inner Radiance
Drawings of the Tögal Visions

Water Drawn Before Sunrise
A Journey of Return

LUMINOUS
HEART
OF THE
EARTH

A Survival Guide
for
Original Heart

Robert *&* Rachel Olds

HEART SEED PRESS

Heart Seed Press

www.acircleisdrawn.org

email: robert.rachel@acircleisdrawn.org

ISBN 978-0-983-1945-9-0

Cover and book design: Robert & Rachel Olds

Homage to luminous inner radiance,
Primordial awakened heart,
Seed of your very being,
Essence beyond concepts,
All encompassing, beyond all that is,
All embracing, beyond going beyond,
Nothing not nothing, spontaneously arising.

CONTENTS

PREFACE

This book is a map laid out in words, a trail guide to a country profoundly outside words, a country from which we as a culture are moving farther and farther away, yet it is still accessible to anyone who feels compelled in their hearts to journey there and make their home. This is a way home, a homesteader's book, a spiritual survival guide for original heart. This began as a text for people who had been practicing Dzogchen for a number of years and who had begun to realize that very little had changed for them and were searching for a deepening of their practice outside ideas and doctrine. But it is for all those who feel an instinctive resonance between spiritual practice and nature, for those who are seeking direct experience of spiritual awakening rather than further ritual or elaboration, and for those who seek a way to deepen their connection with their hearts, who perceive that our intellect-dominated culture has stifled a quality of livingness that they sense has wider dimensions and offers a doorway to profound connection with the wellspring of all life.

We traveled a long road on our personal journey as we made our way back from the fragmentation and separation of modern times in our quest to reclaim the natural wholeness of spiritual practice, life, and Earth. We touched this wholeness in the spontaneous experience of inner radiance arising from our hearts and heard it in the voice of North America, the land itself calling to us, demanding that we recognize the technological and social horrors being engendered here, reminding us that there is another way, the path of Earth and heart blended within the intent of essence, just as it was with the ancient ones as they responded to this primordial call and followed it to its final return.

We spent nine years in retreat together in the mountains of Northern California. For five and a half of those years we lived in a simple pit dwelling that we built in the forest above a Tibetan Buddhist lay monastery. Even after moving to a one-room cabin later in our retreat, the rhythms of hauling water and hiking steep mountain trails continued to shape our daily lives. In this context, we received and practiced the Dzogchen teachings as conveyed through the Tigle Gyachen and the Chetzun Nyingtik cycles. As we approached fruition on the path of Tögal, our teacher urged us to consider writing about our experience and advice for future practitioners in the West. In the resolution of Tögal you go beyond all concepts and doctrine, your philosophical systems fall away. Your perspective is one with the intent of essence. When we began writing after having completed the path of Tögal, we needed to find a way to convey this perspective in language that reflected the direct experience of this primordial expression of essence.

Tögal is a path of return to essence, a blending of your very being into essence, like water into water, only a seamless whole. Immersed in a spontaneous, dynamic visionary process arising from your heart and the very basis of all experience, you enter a path of light at the very edge of essence. The four great visions of Tögal become your teacher just as the Earth has been your teacher since birth, through direct experience of the heart. The practice of Tögal is a profound connection with the living essence manifest in its purest form. The visions arise in the same way and in the same progression for everyone. Although Tögal requires many years of letting go before entering this path and years of day and night practice in retreat, the basis of Tögal is universal, the birthright of all beings, a natural, unconfused path free of the assumptions of language or culture.

Within the oneness of the final resolution of the path, we looked at our lives and the choices we made along the way. As we began to write, we explored the events of our lives that seemed most pivotal for us. We saw a pattern emerging in the events and in the words we chose. Two words in particular, heart and Earth, were pointing to an orientation outside language and doctrine that had enabled us along the path while so many other practitioners around us were having difficulties. When we began to write a guidance manual for Tögal, we focused first on what we considered our true preliminaries, our experiences of the Earth as a teacher and a context for nurturing an aware openness of heart. This is the portion of the text we are offering here, and we consider it the heart of our advice, not only for Tögal practice, but also for authentic spiritual growth on any path. It is crucial to enter into the wilderness, to feel the breadth of that experience through your whole being. The openness of spiritual growth is not conceptual; it is a relationship with the intent of essence. You need to experience openness purely, through the heart, as vivid as the sky, not corrupted by words or thoughts but felt and touched, your very being changed directly, being as sky, being as Earth, moving with, breathing with, one with the experience of life as vision.

We feel a responsibility to the essence, to the visions, and to the Earth to share this part of our heart advice at this time. Throughout our practice of Tögal, we always relied on the Earth as a support and now more than ever, we feel the sacredness of every aspect of this arising vision we call life. Humanity is coming to the end of an age. The seductive blindness of technology and the captivity of the heart continue to grow, destroying our Earth. There is no time to debate, no time to speculate. If our words resonate with your heart, put them into practice; learn to live with our Mother, not just in a physical way, but feeling her through your whole being. This is a survival manual and a prayer for the luminous aware original heart of all life.

PRELUDE TO
A NEW BEGINNING

The smell of the sea, the calm waves lapping at our feet, and the air so alive with a presence of water not yet as bracing or challenging as the full force of the Pacific. We were waiting for a ferry to take us across to one of the San Juan Islands, at the end of our second day out of retreat. The water sounds and the salty moist air were embracing us at our next beginning and the conclusion of another end.

The world had changed dramatically over the nine years we had been in retreat. It was early March of 2006. Small waves lapped at our feet as we stood on a strip of beach near the dock, pondering a peculiar sign at the ferry landing, a chart of colors and levels of alert. We thought that maybe it was for a new kind of weather or storm warning system, or possibly the level of the tide. There was no explanation on the sign. Apparently it was assumed that everyone already knew. The highest level was red, and no one seemed concerned that the level was already at orange, the color just below red. The people milling about as people do while waiting for public transport were talking as if to themselves, talking about what they were seeing or doing or forgetting or remembering, as if to some unseen person who was not there but needed to know everything they were doing. We felt like the main character in the remake of *The Invasion of the Body Snatchers,* wondering if we too should start talking aloud so we would not be noticed or found out.

The ferry finally arrived. We boarded and went to the upper level, a grand gallery with wide windows and upholstered seats, and sat looking out at the last bit of the sun glistening on the even waves. The gallery was very warm. As the ferry left the dock, we settled into the vibration and pulse of the engines and the slow steady progress across the calm channel sea. There were few other passengers. In the deepening twilight, the colors of the glowing sky silhouetted the dark shapes of the islands as we passed. The islands were slowly sinking into water and night like the rounded backs of immense creatures of the sea, with the timeless motions of a dream. A poetic ride, imbued with the mystery of coming into and out of form. A sacred passage over water, within the nurturing hum and warmth of the ferry like a great mother comforting and secure with the heat and rhythm of life.

Shattering the peace of the crossing, the woman sitting close to us pulled out a small plastic device and started speaking loudly. She spoke as if she was on a phone, but unlike anyone we had ever heard talk on a phone before, publicly, insistently, compulsively. She was speaking in earnest detail to the unseen person, completely oblivious to the beauty passing by. We were witnessing a strange illness that seemed to have swept over everyone while we were away.

People all seemed as if they were hiding from something within this incessant talking to the unseen person. It did not matter whom we spoke with later or watched as we sat in our booth crossing, leaving, and coming into another journey. When we finally learned that the alert sign was for terror attacks we were stunned. We had heard about 9/11, but we were shocked at the level of fear and denial that it had induced. A great repression had come over everyone we met, omnipresent, borderless, and so deep that it permeated all levels of behavior and experience both collective and personal, as if covering over a primal horror as deep as knowing that your father, mother, lover, or protector has raped, enslaved, or betrayed you. It was tangible, outside of words; we could feel it.

A few days later, we went into a small electronic store on one of the islands. The salesman was busy with a customer and while we waited for him to finish, we watched with increasing fascination the images moving on a very large flat screen TV at one end of the room. There was no sound accompanying the dreamlike scenes of what appeared to be a recreation of an ancient village in northern Europe. Filmed in golden ethereal light, people in costumes of this far off era were reenacting the skills of that time, slowly, patiently, spinning yarn, weaving cloth, making rope, building boats and simple houses, and forging simple tools. The poetry of their movements and the skills were poignant. The slow pace and simplicity of their way of life resonated with our hearts, so recently out of our long retreat, still held within a world of experience as far away as this earlier time. It was an unexpected reminder and an affirmation of how crucial we feel it is for people to live more gently with the Earth, in harmony rather than in separation from the life that nurtures us. When the salesman came over to speak with us, we turned to him and he said what do you think of that. Pointing at the images on the screen, we said this is wonderful. He said yes, the new technology is amazing, and began rapturously to tell us about flat screens and HDTV.

The natural world is a world that has become remote to the modern age. The simplicity of living with the Earth, so close to our hearts, yet for so many others, far away, is overlooked or locked in some flat screen TV. The slowness, attention, and physicality of life in harmony with the Earth has become distant and inaccessible to people lost in an escalating technological delusion of separation, seeking ever increasing stimulation, sucking the heart out of whatever is left of the natural world. The salesman, for all his good intentions and enthusiasm, was giving voice to how far people had gone, how completely seduced by technology that they cannot see the nightmare unfolding all around them, a nightmare that is destroying the very thing that can set them free and reclaim direct experience and true humanity, the Earth.

The islands drifting on the calm sea, the shrill phone conversations, and the encounter with HDTV were landmarks for some key recognitions along our passage back into our times, times that had moved on so fast while we were away that they had forgotten things that now very much needed remembering.

We both had dreams of radiant tropical landscapes at a defining moment in our practice of Tögal, dreams unexpected in contrast to the familiar landscape of our forest retreat. After spending a year and a half living in seclusion outside Santa Fe, New Mexico, while we worked on our Tögal manual, we were offered the opportunity to live in Costa Rica and build a small retreat cabin on some land that friends had in the mountains there.

Late in the afternoon on the day we arrived in Costa Rica, we found ourselves in a very small, glass walled cabin beside a small lotus pond high in the Talamanca Mountains. We remained beside the pond for two years while we put in an organic garden and built our own cabin farther up the mountain. There were many others standing beside us that first night, the tall bamboos, grasses we did not yet know, the rounded boulders we had seen in our visionary dreams, the flowers dimly showing themselves in the dense foliage all around us, and the lotus and the stars floating together on the pond's surface in the liquid night. The whole sphere of the pond was one with its surroundings, sky and clouds and stars reflecting onto the surface shining in the moonlight, the plants around the water's edge blending with the sky's reflection, and here and there the cream white of a lotus blossom. Heart and sky moving as one, spheres within a spheres.

A few days later, we made our way slowly along the steep trail leading farther up the mountain. As we climbed higher, the houses in the valley below grew smaller and smaller. The roar of the river fell away in the moist air. We passed the sharp ridge of one flank of the mountain and the houses and the river sound were erased, blocked by the tall stands of gigante grass that cloaked the ridge. The slopes around us, no longer grazed, were covered with thickets of bushes and young trees. The forest was reclaiming land that it had been denied for a few short decades. The mountainsides were laden with every imaginable green hue, melting into blue only in far distances. This was a world of living green. The section we were walking through had been logged just twenty years ago, and the land had not forgotten the presence of the forest and the energy that had engendered it.

We rounded a bend in the eroding track that clung precariously to the side of the mountain and came to the edge of the older forest, huge grey columns of trees reaching upward from the depths of time through long vines trailing down from another depth of sky. We stood in awe, rooted in the slow eternal livingness all around us. A sheen of moisture glistened on every surface. Here below the highest canopies so far above was a world of roots and mists and waters, rocks and stone and wet Earth, and a sense of ancient and immense presence. The cloud forests are the most complete expressions of the natural life force of the Earth, clothing the tropical mountains with this profusion of life to buffer the intense energy of the sun at these latitudes. The complexity and harmony of this place was staggering. Life energies came into balance with each other so long ago, the harmonies were given freely now, without disruption, a wisdom of being, natural, unforced. We were standing in the effulgent presence of the third vision of Tögal embodied as the forest, manifest from the same source.

The whole of this wondrous vision we call life is here for us, teaching, pulling, and prodding us to return to essence. From within this world as vision we pray that the sacred teachings arising moment by moment within the natural world will no longer be at the edge of potential ruin, at risk from a westernized world culture that is heading toward collapse, the culmination of its own expansion. We offer this text as a prayer that people will again live from their hearts in harmony with the vision that is this life and allow the generative power of the intent of essence as Earth to flow unhindered and unmolested. We saw in the rain forest the immense vitality of natural life. There is still within the Earth the capacity to regenerate, if humanity is willing to live from the heart in balance with all that naturally arises.

HOW TO USE THIS BOOK

Read the entire book gently, slowly, letting the words flow into your heart, perhaps outdoors in a special place where you feel safe, secure, and whole, or sit with the light on a windowsill; letting the light glow across the pages of the book and read words that are part of the same soft light. After you have read the entire book, begin again at the beginning. Choose a practice or a topic that you feel drawn to and then go outdoors, use our suggestions as an avenue to blend with the vision that is this life. Experience it for yourself, come to know what direct experience is for you, and feel the path growing, not thinking it, but feeling it deep within you, as naturally as light rests on a windowsill, as naturally as a plant sprouts and grows.

Some of the practices are ways of living, suggestions for changing your way of being, such as wide-angle vision, Earth walking, and breaking habits. Others are helpful guides leading to other experiences along the path. Everyone is at a different point on his or her spiritual journey. Openings can come in unexpected ways, but in general, we consider wide-angle vision to be one of the most effective ways to transform your perceptions and your life, and it can facilitate a great number of other openings. Some qualities of experience will be quite noticeable at first; others will be felt more slowly over time. You are reclaiming a forgotten heritage that is intrinsic to the human soul.

This book is meant as a trail guide, a companion. Put it in your backpack; take it outside. It is a prayer that we all live again in harmony and reverence within original heart and the heart of this Earth, blended within the joy that naturally arises from the intent of essence.

INTENT OF ESSENCE

ESSENCE

Pure essence is beyond all aspects of this world, beyond all beliefs, all concepts, all perspectives, and all experience, a luminous knowingless knowing that cannot be defined, a primordial purity that is beyond emptiness and spacious beyond all concepts of space, absolute potential, neither tangible nor intangible, yet its expression is everywhere.

The absolute potential of the essence arises as a dynamic energy, an intent that bursts forth like the corolla of a flower from a blue-black centerless depth. All that we experience, all that we perceive, is this intent radiating out of this depth. Both the radiance and the depth are present in everything and everyone, even the tiniest insect.

RADIANCE

The radiance blossoming forth from the essence, the spontaneous unceasing dynamic expression blooming in myriad ways, is the great compassion. This radiance, this compassion, is not random; it is a direct manifestation of the intent of the essence, an intent for all beings to reflect back to the origin. The specific, compassionate intent that creates the entire world vision we find ourselves within begins with light, a spontaneous continuity of essence and radiance. The light then shapes itself into myriad rainbow colors and countless circles or spheres of being that are free and undefined, yet they form the continuum of all manifest experience as color, shape, and light. The mind defines and labels, changing and reordering its perception of what is naturally manifest into the holding patterns of time and space. Then this realm of light appears as the spatially defined and bordered solidities of the familiar world. But at the same time that the mind is structuring its experience, you are still living within the realm of rainbow circles of light.

The circular shape is also a movement, just as a circle is drawn. This movement is an expression of the cyclical nature of radiance as a path of return from the point of origin. It is the basis for the path of Tögal and it shapes all manifestation. Once a circle is drawn from a single point, where is the beginning, where is the end? In the energy of a line sweeping upward, around and curving down to merge seamlessly with itself, the completion is inherent in the beginning. Circles from the point of origin are apparent everywhere: bubbles form on water in a light rain; rainbows bloom in a misty sky; seeds sprout, grow upward, mature and set seed again; waters flow in rivulets and mountain streams into larger rivers leading to the sea, then rise into sky and clouds, and fall as rain on mountaintops again. A luminous seed or sphere of this sacred cycle is in the heart of every being, waiting to be awakened and return you to essence through the field of natural manifestation all around you and within you.

The expression of this world as the intent of essence does not arise as an illusion to deceive. It does not arise as delusion to make us suffer, or to drive us to turn away or escape. Nor is it just a dream to be seduced by or to be tossed aside. This expression of the essence is a vision, a sacred vision with a living intent woven into the fabric of our being.

Within this radiant vision we call the world, everything is already naturally consecrated as an expression of the essence. The Earth, trees, plants, rivers, clouds, and sky, colors, odors, tastes, textures, and sounds, all manifestations of the essence, large and small, partake of the source from which they arise. The brilliance and the core essence are never separate. This unity is beyond time or space, beyond concepts, yet it can be seen, experienced, felt, responded to, and recognized, to complete the reflection of its return.

The arising brilliance of this world as an expression of a pure intent can be seen and felt most clearly in the natural world outside human manipulation. The signs of this radiance are everywhere: in the night sky, in a rainbow, in the sun and moon, in the elemental interplay of water, fire, Earth, wind, and space. This natural brilliance is also found within your heart, and just as the marvel of a seed settles in a nurturing bed of soil, sprouting, growing, and transforming, the luminous seed of the essence already settled in your heart can also sprout and grow, initiating the particular cycle of return that is the path of Tögal, the path of the visions of inner radiance. Yet the qualities of inner radiance are also here now all around us abundantly in this world, in the spontaneously arising nature of our experience, and it is important to recognize and experience these qualities to progress along any spiritual path.

The natural world is a fluid movement. Interrelated cycles of change appear as the arising and fading rhythms of experience, and similar to bubbles on the surface of a pond, these manifest phenomena have no power to remain, due to the ceaseless transitory nature of their arising. And so the splendor of this life also includes decline and decay; they are natural necessary aspects of the cycles of change just as composting builds rich soil.

Everything that manifests in our experience, the joys and the difficulties, the choices and the ability to choose, are all expressions of the compassion of the essence. Great compassion is a fertile dynamic environment for growth. Hot and cold, up and down, near and far, fast and slow, night and day, birth and death, Earth and sky, are all aspects of the manifest dance of the essence moving us to return. The complementary forces all around us provide support within which we learn and grow. The problem is not the dualistic quality of our experience; the problem is holding and clinging with our minds to any part of this dynamic whole, hindering the natural fluidity of the interactions and restricting the potential for growth.

Holding and clinging arise from an illusory sense of separation, the ignorance that manifests as self-identity. All beings have a personal sphere of being, an avenue through which they experience and choose, and are part of the great primordial compassion at the same time. The lack of recognition of this inherent unity leads to clinging and the feeling of separation. The cycle is never ending, unless you embrace a spiritual path of letting go that cleans and polishes the inner surface of your sphere until it becomes open like the sky. Then, like the rainbow surface of a bubble growing thinner and thinner, it pops, and there is no more sphere, only a seamless all.

This whole world is a sacred vision, the radiance of the essence arising naturally, spontaneously, here, abundantly, and within this abundance every being has the potential to let go of separation and return to the unity of original heart. It is here for you to touch, it is calling you. The only reason we are here is to heed this call to return. And so, an important step on any spiritual path is taking responsibility for your thoughts and actions, for how you respond to the miraculous vision we call this world, taking responsibility to undo the patterns of separation that hold you and regain the connection that has been covered over but never really lost, to recognize and nurture the seed of radiance in your heart.

OPENNESS OF EARTH

Ask yourself, what is your purpose in this life? What would you be willing to do to truly follow the teachings of the essence to the ultimate goal of realizing what is already abiding in your heart, coming to the point of complete union with it, no separation, the dissolution of all concepts, habitual patterns, and emotions? How strong is your intent to traverse the full length of the path for all beings, for all life, for every aspect of this amazing vision, not only for yourself?

The intent to benefit outside of self is crucial for the spiritual path. As natural as the caring of a mother for her child, this intent is already within you whether you are a man or a woman. You do not have to take a vow; just accept right now, right where you are, that this nurturing quality is indwelling in your heart, and allow it to radiate outward for all life. This inherent kindness is the same as the functional underlying kindness of the intent of the essence manifesting as the Earth, and this kindness includes the ripening of whatever seed is sown. Selfish actions and motivations bring conditions of increasing separation and arrested spiritual growth. Many people in western cultures are afraid of the Earth, afraid of directly experiencing the elemental aspects of life, and afraid of confronting the results of their choices and actions as reflected back to them by the Earth; they prefer the illusion of autonomy and cut themselves off from the depth of the nurturing quality abiding within.

To progress along the path, we need to realize in our hearts that we are one with the Earth, and we need to be able to surrender to the faithful, kindly energies already in our hearts. We need to recognize and accept that there is a kindness of intent here, both in the Earth and in our hearts. This intent expresses itself through the same qualities traditionally attributed to the Earth that are the very attributes of your heart that you need to recognize and cultivate for the seed of awakened heart to grow, bloom, and set the seed of fruition.

The Earth responds dynamically, naturally abundant and effulgent. Although we tend to experience the Earth as solid and firm ground, the actual growing layer of the soil is in a continually responsive, fertile state of transformation. The Earth is unconditional openness, allowing any choice to bear fruit. The Earth is unwavering devotion, nurturing all appearances as expressions of the essence. The Earth is absolute humility, receptive to all. These attributes of Earth, responsive, accepting, devoted, and humble are interactive and mutually supportive. They are all qualities of a fundamental receptive openness that is a natural aspect of the essence and is all pervasive within the manifest world. It is present here for you to recognize and learn from. It is particularly evident in the Earth, and it is already in your heart. Just as the intent to benefit outside of self is a reflection of the larger intent of the essence, the receptive openness that you can feel within the Earth and in your heart is a direct connection with the essence, and once it is recognized it can be cultivated through the choices you make in your life.

RESPONDING

Being receptive is not being passive; it is an active willingness to relate with the radiance of the essence, the whole of experience that is manifesting ceaselessly, outwardly and inwardly. It is a direct response from your heart, a direct involvement with the very fabric of our world. The willingness to respond is the basis for taking responsibility for the choices you make and learning from them, taking responsibility for being part of the Earth, taking responsibility for your own life and responding to the myriad lives around you with a nurturing heart.

ALLOWING

This responding leads naturally to a fluid, allowing mind, soft and gentle, that does not hold or grasp onto situations, concepts, habits, and emotions and does not deny or cling. This mind is willing to listen to and follow the heart. It is willing to allow the heart to be open like the Earth, accepting anything and everything without judgment. The Earth is an absolute mother willing to allow her children to discover and experience so that they can truly learn, even though they may cause her great pain, and it takes a while to develop a truly allowing mind that will accept and participate with that level of openness. You start by breaking habits, letting go of grasping and holding, and as energies no longer bound up in holding or fixating become available, you come more and more to the natural generosity of the indwelling openness of your heart.

DEVOTION

The Earth is an expression of the intent of the essence; it arises as a support for all beings to return. As you touch this unwavering reciprocal intent of Earth and essence, you realize that everything is a teacher. A loving commitment and respect arise naturally as a profound trust in the essence and its countless manifestations. The devotion of the essence for all to return is seen in the elemental equally loving commitment of gravity, air, soil, plants, water, fire, and space, and the devotion arising in your heart for the Earth and the essence is also a reflection of the same intent guiding you through all appearances. This natural devotion gives the ability to bond and relate, to accept grace, to relinquish control and surrender.

True devotion is not obedience to a human authority or a hierarchy of doctrine. It is not meant to be a feudal state. The mind plays a strong role in keeping you subject to the minds and ideas of others; if you let your mind become a tyrant this sets up a willingness to delegate authority to external structures. You do not want to surrender your responsibility, your ability to respond, to your mind or to another person. This does not mean that you do not have respect for spiritual guides; it means that you recognize your responsibility for your own journey and that the ultimate source of the path is the essence itself manifesting all around you in the natural world. You do not need to rely on human interpretation to meet the intent of the essence in the natural world and in your heart. Devotion is about opening your heart to the soul of all that manifests naturally.

HUMILITY

Giving yourself wholeheartedly, surrendering to the pull of the essence in your heart without any structure or any knowing how to do it, is humility. True humility is not submitting to a doctrine or following the rules. It is very subtle. It involves no new identity, no new status. You are empty; you give up yourself completely, outside hierarchy or achievement. The basic ground of spiritual practice is a feeling, a living wholeness; you just float in your humility, open and surrendering. When your mind lets go, steps out of the way and relinquishes control, you see clearly from your heart that you are already part of the oneness of the intent of the essence. As you allow the purpose of your heart to lead you, you simplify your life and bring your wants and needs down to nothing, and then all that comes to you is more than enough. This ancient way of being, respectful and gentle, is the nurturing ground from which all spiritual growth arises.

Responding, allowing, devotion, and humility lead to an allowing mind that is open to the natural knowing in your heart, reverent and humble, touching and relating with the basis of this existence. But along with recognizing these qualities of the Earth within your heart, we cannot emphasize enough how living closer to the physical Earth, the actual ground of this life, knowing how to live and meditate upon and with our first mother, is crucial to the path that brings us to the ultimate open luminous heart of inner radiance.

LETTING GO

The Earth is the basic ground on which our lives and our spiritual practice evolve. It is the intent of the essence manifesting for all beings to seek and find the path of return. This expression of the essence is like a dream, although it appears as if solid and real. All experience, all phenomena, are as evanescent as a mist in the midday sun, but this does not in any way diminish the inherent holiness of this manifest vision we call life. The whole of this wondrous world arises for us to follow the signs guiding, opening, and gentling us, helping us let go and surrender to the embrace of the essence. This vision of Earth is meant to be directly experienced, to feel the pulse of our Mother within and without, to make a deep connection with the attributes that are here for us to emulate. The openness of the sky, the fluidity of water, the perseverance of mountains, the responsive, accepting, devoted, and humble qualities of Earth are here for us to witness, feel, touch, and experience with our whole being, so that they become alive within us and we recognize and accept our indwelling heritage.

To enter into the allowing openness of our hearts we need to come into direct experience of the sacred nature of the Earth, the spontaneously arising vision of awakened heart, the essence of being. When you begin to really feel and interact with the energies and blessings all around you, your heart will open naturally. To do this we need to break down the barriers that keep us separate from the natural world. Once the wilderness was no longer the context of our daily lives, we set up new contexts, artificial constructs both physical and mental, and once these were in place we had to hold to and maintain them. When you hold to anything, there is a fear that if it breaks down you will be lost. We have forgotten how to trust and embrace the Earth as our home. If you know the most basic survival skills, how to build a simple shelter of natural materials, how to make fire without flint or matches, how to find water and identify a few medicinal and edible plants, if you know how to live with our mother the Earth, you are no longer afraid on a most basic, primal level. This gives you a deep trust in the Earth and in yourself that allows the natural openness of your heart to unfold.

You do not have to become an expert in survival skills. The Earth skills for original heart are very simple, although they require letting go of many habits of mind and body. This is the greater part of the work for people raised in the modern world, as well as being a necessary aspect of the spiritual path at any time. Letting go of habits and experiencing the sacredness and generosity of the Earth will allow the indwelling openness of your heart to grow. We want to share some practices that helped move us to deeper recognition of the natural openness of our hearts. We offer them as prayers that others may enhance their personal experience of this sacred fluid vision we call Earth and nurture an open heart blossoming like a flower.

The teachings surround you in the natural world; let go into the stream of nature, enter into what you already have, a heart of radiant joy ready to embrace and be embraced by the essence. The truth surrounds you in nature, and if your heart is open, you will be taught.

EARTH SITTING

The Earth is the temple of the holy ones. If all the texts and written words were to disappear, you would still be surrounded and embraced by the teachings that are naturally present in this manifest world. So many of the spiritual metaphors that have come down to us in writing are based on direct expressions of the essence arising all around us. Openness is not like the sky, it is one with the sky, it is the sky. Fluidity is not like water, it is one with water, it is water. They are participatory, not conceptual. Wherever you are, the land itself is the actual basis of your spiritual practice. Listen to the voices of the winds, the waters, the rocks, the plants, and the trees. They form the great song within which all other voices, human, bird, insect, and animal, are woven into a whole.

Go outdoors reverently, quietly, as if entering a shrine. Experience the wonders of this Earth with the innocence of a child. Sit for a while without expectations, watching cloud shapes billowing, growing, and spreading across the sky, then dissolving into a blue expanse. Sit on a mountain, seeing mountain, feeling mountain, being mountain, entering into the strength of the rocks and trees. Sit with a pond or a small stream, feel the fluidity of water in motion and in stillness. Sit on a beach or a cliff above the sea, feel the depth and immensity of ocean as being. Sit on a cliff looking out at an unobstructed blue sky or lie down and blend your whole being with the vastness overhead. Sit through the night waiting for the dawn or lay down on the Earth watching the stars pass over you. Witness the passage of the sun and moon and feel their movement within you.

Wherever you are, you can deepen your experience by keeping your body calm and relaxed. When walking, move slowly and quietly; when sitting, do not move after you have settled in. The most effective and traditional way to sit in openness and enter the subtle field of resonance of Earth and heart is to sit on the Earth, cross-legged, full lotus, half lotus, or in a more open cross-legged posture. If you are accustomed to any of these ways of sitting with only a small cushion or directly on the Earth, you can sit anywhere, at any time, you do not need to bring a lot of equipment with you. The essential part of any posture is to keep your back upright but relaxed in its natural curves and your shoulders relaxed as well. This allows your subtle energy to move smoothly and helps you settle your mind and stay calm and alert. Your eyes are open but not focusing on anything in your field of vision. Breathe gently and evenly. Keep your chin tucked in a little bit and relax your jaw. Place the tip of your tongue to the roof of your mouth right behind your teeth to allow an even flow of the energies that arise while you practice. Relax into the posture, with a glimmer of a smile reflected in your eyes and mouth.

This inner smile comes easily if you have a real appreciation for the hospitality of the spot you are sitting on, for its relatedness with you, the oneness of all life within the essence manifesting right here now. Once you have settled into the posture and the place do not move. Do not shift your eyes. Allow your subtle and physical energies to slow down.

Rest your speech in silence, and keep your breath soft and smooth, melting, blending, merging your responsiveness with the responsiveness of the Earth, not wandering off to the past or the future, but returning to whatever arises in your present experience. Keep your eyes from wandering also, settling your eyes gently, allowing the whole visual field all at once, until your eyes are sky-like, still, and vast. Your silence will blend with the space you have allowed, and your breath will slow and soften as if becoming the rhythmic pulse of a calm sea, the shallow even waves merging with the slope of the beach and elongating until the sound is hushed. If your being stirs and wanders then bring it back to this moment, peaceful and open, recognizing that you are part of the expansive vision unfolding around you.

DIRECT PERCEPTION

Direct perception is from the heart. You were born with the capacity for direct experience. Your heart is already waiting like a small lamp deep in the woods. You can sense its warmth, and maybe see the glow up ahead. Your heart will call to you if you are open to hearing its voice. All that separates us from our hearts are the elaborations created by our minds. Too often people experience the world secondhand with their perception clouded by a frenetic information overload. We as a species have allowed our intellect to take control and condemn or dismiss our hearts. Many people do not have any real sense of the value of the heart. We need to begin to break away from all the constraints of the mind, to move past the hold our minds have on our perception.

You may have had a brief glimpse of an aware openness that is beyond what you normally experience. Maybe it brought tears to your eyes and you prayed that you could re-experience it, perhaps by repeating it through your memory of how it happened originally, yet it does not return. Direct perception is a function of the heart; it arises organically, naturally. You must enter the heart of the vision that is this life, connect with it through your own heart, then experience the openings that this connection brings, openings into a world that is alive, arising, flowing, teaching you with its movement outside of words. Direct perception is a visionary world of experience opening up to you moment by moment out of the intent of the essence. You begin to move and experience within a flow, a fluid ongoing sense of awakening guided by this call. It is in the sound of water, the morning light in the trees, the movement of grasses in the wind. Direct perception is this flow of being, a generative feeling blended with all feeling, the expression of the essence within you and within all experience. Direct perception is not the same as so-called objective observation by the mind. Direct perception is the true nature of experience revealed through the heart.

WIDE-ANGLE VISION

Wide-angle vision is a powerful support for opening your heart as you sit or as you walk. Just as openness is the natural mode of your heart, wide-angle vision is the natural mode of your eyes. Original peoples used their eyes in wide-angle vision most of the time, using more tightly focused tunnel vision only for specific tasks. The modern world with its emphasis on the written word demands focused tunnel vision for most activities. It has become a habit even when not necessary, and this use of the eyes in turn reinforces tunnel mind, restricted and closed to other modes of perception. Learning to use the eyes in wide-angle vision, aware without focusing on the peripheral field, allows the mind to open to the natural spaciousness of the heart and eyes.

The mind or intellect is closely connected to the eyes. Wide-angle vision allows all the imagery in a 180 degree range to come in at once, and this saturation of the visual field floods the brain with information. This shifts attention to the incoming receptive quality of the eyes, to receptiveness itself rather than content. This softens the intensity of the mind and lessens its ability to control the heart. Wide-angle vision can help cut through the mind's tendency to take over, and you can settle into your heart. Because it is the natural way to use our eyes, this is a very effective way for modern spiritual practitioners to reclaim direct experience of the natural indwelling openness of our hearts.

The physical eye is a vast microcosm of elemental forces of water and light. Light passes through this living sea going both ways. There is a fluid power to the eyes that reaches out and connects with what it sees. It can meet, hold, push, or pull at need. If this power is guided by the mind, it grabs and pulls back into itself and interprets in ways that reinforce perceptions upholding separate identity. The eyes can also be used more purely, to connect with and relate from the heart, and with this more open use of the eyes, seeing becomes a mutual embrace as you embrace your experience and are in turn embraced.

Most people have allowed their minds to be dominant and use their eyes in a channeled, tunnel vision way, not only through habitually focusing on the written word, but also by grabbing blindly out of the negative emotions and limitations of separate identity upheld by the mind. This experience of the mind can be very compelling, making it difficult to access the natural inclusiveness and openness of your heart. Wide-angle vision can help release the hold that the mind has on the eyes and on the heart. Your eyes go naturally into wide-angle vision when you go to your heart, and the process is reciprocal; intentionally going into wide-angle vision facilitates blending with your heart.

EARTH WALKING

Find a good area or a trail that is private, and walk very, very slowly and quietly. The point is not to concentrate on going slow, but to allow the slowness to open all your senses, to expand your perception and not tunnel in. Use your feet to slow yourself down. Walk barefoot or in flexible thin-soled shoes with little or no heel, feeling the Earth meet your foot at each step. In the ancient way of Earth walking, you shift out of the headlong heel-first movements of our rushing world into the more respectful, balanced cadence of walking as a prayer of openness. Placing each foot gently, slowly, you touch the ground first with the outside of your foot, then roll the weight of your foot toward the instep, onto the ball, then place the heel, then the toes. This frees your movements from reliance on your eyes; you sense the ground with your feet instead, not placing your full weight until you really feel the ground beneath your foot and any twigs, leaves, or pebbles there. This receptive way of walking helps you to slow down and walk very quietly, blending with the life around you.

Allow your movements to be fluid and graceful. It may seem awkward at first, but as the rhythms of this way of walking become more natural for you, you move more and more like ripples across still water, melting effortlessly into the whole. With your sight resting lightly on the horizon ahead of you, keep your eyes in wide-angle vision, aware without focusing on whatever appears at the edge of your field of vision. As you walk in this way with wide-angle vision, the world seems to flow by and the naturally molten quality of all experience becomes more evident. Slow walking in wide-angle vision shifts ordinary patterns of motion and time and allows entrance into a more expansive sense of openness. It will also connect you to subtle perceptions not only of the physical world but of the spirit world as well. Especially when you do this practice at night, it will intensify your awareness of the good and bad energies of the different areas you are moving through, giving you an inner experience of the spirit energies that can linger on the land, a valuable knowing for living within this shared vision.

WAITING FOR ANIMALS

Sit in an area that feels good and inviting, calm your body and mind, and wait for animals. When you go for a walk, pay attention to the movements of animals, follow the patterns of birds, learn the activities of insects and fish, then find a spot nearby where you can be close to these rhythms, using the whole experience to settle into your heart, with a knowing in your silent presence that you are a part of this arising vision. Once you have settled in, the animals, birds, and insects will slowly resume their own natural flow of activity all around you. It takes time for both you and the animals to calm down. Almost everyone has felt the blessing in the unexpected approach of a large or small free animal or bird, and the spontaneous openness, respect, and gratitude for the gift of this trust. When animals come close to you, still your beating heart and soften your tightening breath so you do not scare them away. Stay with openness and gratitude, keeping your eyes in wide-angle vision. Animals will feel the focus of your eyes, and your mind and your eyes will be reflected in the way they act around you.

Sitting and waiting quietly for animals, keeping your eyes in wide-angle vision as an animal comes closer, is good training for recognizing the power of your eyes and how you are using them. Just as animals will feel the quality of your eyes, you will feel the quality of their eyes as well. Animals can also reach out with their eyes, and they are very sensitive to this use. They will bolt if your eyes grab onto to them in an ordinary way. Training in wide-angle vision while waiting for animals helps develop reverent eyes that connect naturally with the allowing openness of your heart. Waiting for animals is a profound training for your whole being; it is a practice of opening to the approach of grace, and the skills you develop in this way are vital for the spiritual path and especially for Tögal, which is a practice of the approach of grace in a very pure form.

In addition to providing a focal point for calming your mind and body and settling into your heart, waiting for animals allows you to experience the interrelatedness of all life in a very direct way. Once you have settled into a spot and the animals, birds, and insects around you have resumed their own rhythms, you can witness countless subtle interactions. A hawk calls; a small animal holds very still. A butterfly glides through a patch of sunlight; a deer steps out into the open in the same clearing. They are all taking cues from each other, weaving patterns of caution and ease. Like concentric rings expanding outward on the surface of water, the echoes of their actions constantly radiate and intertwine. You feel firsthand the truly dynamic quality of the oneness of all beings as manifestations of the same essence and the same life of the Earth. We are all born of the same mother; we are all brothers and sisters, literally. Communication is ongoing and seamless, whether we hear them or not, the voices of our relatives are everywhere. The personal lives of animals unfolding around you are also reflections within the intent of the essence at the same time, and in the intricate beauty of a flower or the rippling music of a mountain stream, you see another expression of the essence embracing all.

GOOD SPOTS BAD SPOTS

As you settle into the feelings and rhythms of the Earth with your heart, you will be more sensitive to good and bad energies in the areas that you come across. You may feel that some places have a special responsive quality, while others may seem hostile. These are not random energies. The circumstances for their arising may sometimes involve human activity, but areas may also have a deep-seated tone within the fabric of the Earth that has drawn other positive or negative experiences to that spot.

In any given area, there will be specific feelings that speak to you. It is best to focus on positive sites that are willing to provide beneficial energy and circumstances for your practice. A good spot that you have approached respectfully and that is welcoming you is an invitation for a union of intent. But some spots, although they may look sublime and welcoming, may turn out to be the opposite. When practicing in such areas, you might find your mind becoming increasingly agitated, turning toward negative thoughts or extreme emotions, when just a few moments before you were at peace. Wherever you go, pay attention to what the land is telling you. If you choose to sit, once you have settled into a spot, notice how you feel. If you begin to feel unusually restless, uneasy, edgy, or disturbed, you may want to get up and go somewhere else. Be aware of where this feeling is coming from. Has the spot reminded you of an argument you have had, or a personal fear, or are you feeling the residues of other beings' arguments or fears left there? Perhaps you are feeling the place itself, or the territorial warnings from an anthill or a bird's nest nearby, or perhaps a spirit, good, bad, or neutral, lives there. It is important to read the energy of an area accurately so that you can choose the energy you want to be with. Most people already have a feeling for this, and can develop and refine an even subtler sensitivity. Even on a good spot your mind may bring up its own negativities. You need to look honestly at the feelings arising from within and around you and be able to distinguish them. All experiences are teachers, supplying valuable information for the wordless knowing in your body and heart that will help guide you in the future.

Later as your practice of Earth sitting deepens, you may choose to experience bad spots intentionally, to enrich and strengthen your resolve toward an open heart as a prayer for all life, a prayer for all beings to recognize their original heart. It is important to have a purpose vast in scope, outside of self, at all times, but especially when you are practicing with a bad spot. This practice is also best done with a group at first or with an experienced guide.

A HEART PLACE

For anyone with currently heavy emotions, or deep burdens from past lives, or scars from intense experiences that happened in childhood or later, you need to find an especially good spot in nature that you feel a strong connection with, that responds to you and wants to help you, that makes you feel safe, secure, and comforted, a mother energy, a heart place. You do not need the forceful energies of a shaman spot or the challenges of a negative spot. Many people in modern cultures have heavy issues with their mothers in this life, in part because these cultures do not support nurturing mothering energies in general and consider them of lesser value. The Earth is outside those constraints and offers nurturing freely. Everyone needs a place to connect with this nurturing energy at times that are particularly trying, intense, and challenging. You need to feel the landscape and know in your heart the kind of qualities that are there. You need to feel totally safe, protected, and nurtured. You need the loving, embracing, reliable, comforting, unconditional acceptance that the Earth can give you. Whatever heavy burden you are carrying, just sit down in wide-angle vision and gratitude and let the Earth absorb the weight of your emotions, memories, or the leaden burdens of past lives. You do not have to think about them, or work through some psychological process, or direct a flow of energy. You do not have to push the heaviness away, just let the weight of it sink, let the grace of gravity absorb the heaviness. Just sit and give yourself and your burden to the Earth. A heart place connects your heart directly to the heartbeat of the essence manifesting as the Earth. The natural brightness at your heart is like a small candle flame touching another larger flame as you sit with the Earth on a heart place. As the shadow of the burden falls away, you feel the warmth and light at your heart that is naturally there and feel it embraced by the larger warmth and light of the Earth.

This may take some time if your burden is long held, but if you sit repeatedly with a heart place it will slowly be absorbed, and you will be able to let go of more and more of the weight. Difficult memories will not completely fade away, but the deep holding will slowly be released. A heart place is an upwelling of love that will dissolve the burden you are releasing, freeing the indwelling love and nurturing already in your heart to radiate out to others, and as your caring extends beyond yourself, the heaviness and holding will fade away even more.

BLINDFOLDED WALKING

Walking blindfolded outdoors with the slow soft rhythms of Earth walking is a beautiful way to quiet your mind and open your heart. Without the boundaries maintained by your eyes, you perceive the world in a very different way. You can walk following a string that you touch lightly, or on a trail that is obvious in a tactile way to your feet, or with tall grass or thick underbrush on either side, whatever you need to feel confident of your route. Any branching side trails can be closed off with string. You want an area and a route that feel safe to you so that you can move freely, surrendering to the flowing movements of the slow walk, surrendering to the timelessness hidden behind ordinary perception.

Normally, we hold strongly to our sense of the outer world with our eyes. The way things look, solid and real, distant or near, are all upheld by the way the brain reads the information from our eyes. The eyes connect with both voluntary and involuntary nervous systems, so how you use your eyes affects your responses to your experience on many levels. You can loosen the hold that the mind has on your perceptions by blindfolding and allowing other senses to open out. You begin to perceive light directly without using your eyes. You become more aware of the presence of trees, bushes, and the space around you. You may experience a sense of knowing exactly where the trail is. Some people will see in their inner eye a path that glows, and other people may just know in their hearts that they are going in the right direction.

For this deepening of experience, allow yourself several hours at a time to do the practice. Walking blindfolded, moving so slowly, shuts down all concepts of motion. Flowing and continuous, with no coming or going, no here or there, you become one with your experience arising moment by moment. Eventually, after several hours of moving in this non-moving way, you can take off your blindfold and keeping your eyes in wide-angle vision, continue to allow yourself along the trail, vast as space, a knowing that is form in movement, nothing more.

BREAKING HABITS

In order to let go fully, opening to your senses, opening to your heart, you need to break habits of personal identity as well as habits of perception. We are all accustomed to certain ways of being, certain routes we take, certain ways of doing things in our daily lives, and over time they become restrictive, inhibiting us and blinding us to our original heart. Habits can help some aspects of life go more smoothly, but the lack of attention fostered by routines and the accompanying false sense of the stability of objects, situations, and times covers over the freshness and immediacy through which the essence is most clearly seen shining within its manifestations.

To go beyond habitual tendencies you need to want to let them go. You can start by letting go of little things. Choose an activity you do every day, such as brushing your teeth with your right hand, or putting your left shoe on first, and then do the opposite. Breaking a habit may be awkward or humorous at first, but over time, it will become automatic. At this point, drop the new habit and go back to your original way of doing things, then pick another habit to change. Gradually choose larger and larger habits. Do this over a period of years. Though the changes may seem curious and whimsical at first, if you persist, they bring about a very subtle but profound shift in your way of being. You are making an end run around your mind. You begin to see through all habits and patterns of holding, and you are not so bound by them, which engenders a new kind of freedom. Letting go of habits willingly or playfully gives you a confidence in your ability to change; you will be lighter and freer. Like ice returning to water, no longer fixed and rigid, becoming fluid and flexible, you will be less compelled by the story of your identity, "I always", "I never", and so forth. The categories of who you think you are lose their intensity and the habit of self and its demands have less effect on you.

Heading into times of great change it is very helpful to shift habits voluntarily before they are shifted for you. It makes it easier to cope with big changes in a constructive and creative way if you are not held down by your habits, by how things ought to be.

NIGHT SIT

To sit through the night on a good spot and wait for the dawn can pull you out of your habitual world very directly by plunging you into the night's presence. Sitting alone within the immensity and the darkness of the night you are faced with the depth of the unknowable. Boundaries fall away. You are aware of the frailty of your existence. Starlight touches you with the vast distances of space. Moonlight softens all details, turning the familiar landmarks of your world into fragile shells of shadow and pale light. Surrendering to the silence and darkness of the night, you merge with a vastness, delicate and ephemeral as star shine, seamless as the night itself mirroring the depth of the essence beyond radiance.

The night covers over so much of what we habitually experience through light, but the sense of hearing, the tactile knowing of skin, and inner experience of the heart are all enhanced. You are more sensitive to the energies in the area where you are sitting, not only of the land itself and the plants, but also the feelings of the beings moving within the landscape, the animals of the night and the shades of tensions wandering on their desires.

Sitting with the night opens your mind beyond your ordinary perceptions and expands into a deeper experience of your heart touching a livingness all around you that becomes palpable. Even the darkness is alive. As you wait within the silent presence of the night, shedding all that blinds you to this expanded vision, remaining with the night, your heart opens like a prayer flowing over the Earth. Blending with the night, motivated by your purpose for all beings to recognize the essence within themselves, you can touch the stars in your heart. Your mind will let go as your heart expands more and more, just as the dawn will surely come.

DEATH

Any time you sit alone, and particularly in the night, you may come to feel the presence of your inevitable death. Everything that manifests passes away again in an ongoing process. Each moment, each breath, encompasses whole worlds, whole cycles of creation and dissolution. Death is a constant companion; death is part of any change. Acceptance on a deep level of the natural presence of death allows the entire range of energies and life processes to move more freely and the essence to manifest more directly in your experience. Acknowledging death gives you an ability to accept loss and grief as part of the creative process of life. You will not get stuck in the frustration of holding to lost loved ones or lost opportunities in the past, and you will be more open to new situations, not afraid of where they will lead or if they will last. Especially, a feeling that your own death can come at any moment can heighten your livingness now.

Death is part of how the intent of the essence manifests and how you learn, how you do anything in this world. The problems and fears that come up are due to denial of the basic underlying dynamics of this experience. How you feel about death is an indicator of how you relate to the changes of transformation. Death is not a concept; it is an active agent in the cycle of life. Death is a passage to another life, a very fundamental expression of the intent of essence. Access this feeling, this poignant, ephemeral aspect of all life; touch it within your whole being, then your self-important mind that deals in certainties will let go of its hold over your heart. The mind will no longer be the controlling factor in your life, and its role will diminish to its natural function as a simple tool to be used when needed. As it relinquishes its hold, this will also help to break up ideas or concepts of immortality. Feeling that you are immortal gives you a sense that you have plenty of time. You solidify your experience and become cut off from the ephemeral arising nature of life and the lessons that it offers. A feeling of immortality dulls the sense of urgency that you need for the spiritual path. Death is a true friend. Sitting with the night and your inevitable death clarifies your relationship to the intent and the purpose in your heart, helps you touch the intent at the core of your very being, teaching your mind to stand down and allow the heart to flourish.

SIMPLIFING YOUR LIFE

All living beings have habitual patterns, and humans not only have personal patterns but complex cultural patterns as well. Many of these larger patterns are revealing themselves to be very destructive to the Earth. As you develop momentum for changing habits you may also want to consider making larger changes in how you live, cutting back on or disengaging from some modern practices such as electrical power, petroleum products, defecating in water, chemical agriculture, GMO, processed or packaged foods, technologies based on rare earths, and so forth, out of respect for our Mother. These changes may come naturally as renunciation grows within you, or they may be in relation to breaking habits and an awareness of death, but no matter how you come to them, they are potent and much needed prayers.

In our modern world of accelerating mental complexity, the underlying ground of our experience is often obscured. Awareness, inner radiance, clear light, original heart, the radiant depth is not reached through conceptual systems, but through direct experience of the depth itself. This aware presence as it shines out moment by moment from within the arising vision we call life is not accessed by increasing elaboration, but through simplifying your life to be open to the subtlety of its call.

Graceful or difficult, your whole life, the sum of all your choices and perceptions, is already a spiritual path. You can choose to further complicate your life and accumulate more elaborations of the mind, or you can simplify to better hear the voice of the heart of essence reflected in the heart of all life. For many practitioners this is a reason to seek time apart in retreat, and you may find yourself in a formal retreat setting at some point in your journey, but the real work of spiritual growth does not start there. The momentum of all your experience up to the moment you enter retreat is an integral part of the process, and has a great deal to do with why you are there and why you stay even through the hard parts. True retreat begins long before you enter a cloistered space in time for any kind of spiritual practice. The spiritual path is a long journey. What you bring, or perhaps most importantly, what you do not bring to retreat has a strong bearing on the outcome. The time for simplifying your life is now, in the midst of your everyday livingness.

RENUNCIATION

True renunciation is not something you force yourself to do; it comes of itself, after years and years of practice, after letting go of attachments to habits and emotions and recognizing the connection between yourself and the essence. Letting go cuts through aspects of life that you take for granted, and over the years, you find the space that was once filled by habits and elaborations is now open and free. You feel more sense of connection with all life, less separation, more openness; there is less in the way. Slowly you begin to let go of bigger chunks of habitual tendencies. You walk away from them easily, smoothly, without looking back. This renunciation is a way of being that arises out of your heart once you have begun to polish your personal sphere of experience. It comes naturally out of the joy within this grand vision arising to fulfill its own reflection, with an openness and fluidity that allow more and more space within which spiritual awareness can grow and be felt and experienced. And as more habits of mind are dropped aside, you are filled in return by the growing responsiveness of your heart.

As openness and fluidity grow stronger, be careful not to weaken your experience by putting it into words too soon, either to yourself or to others. This is not about keeping secrets but about honoring the new within and allowing your heart the space to grow and blossom without being shaped or stunted by words and concepts. It is about renouncing the need to reinforce identity or solidify the process of change with new stories of becoming. Spiritual growth is an art; you are letting a new dimension of your spiritual life unfold. It is like being in a studio, allowing a piece of artwork to gestate in its own way. If you reach a point at which you really need to speak about your experience or spiritual life, speak with someone with whom you have a deep heart connection, or go outside to a heart place and talk to the Earth, talk to a tree; they know about patience and slow steady growth, they know about the silence of strong roots.

OFFERINGS

Along with letting go of habits, letting go of possessions and giving them to others is a wonderful way to support and energize your spiritual life. The size or amount does not matter; it could be a small portion of your lunch offered to a sparrow, but this giving, however simple, can profoundly open you. Whenever we were about to move or make a change in our lives we made offerings. Even when we had few belongings, we still made offerings when we moved. Our offerings were not only prayers for spiritual growth, but also prayers for the harmony of all life. They were prayers of gratitude to this unfolding sacred vision, gratitude for the beauty around us and the chance to follow the lessons being imparted to us at every step of this journey. The offerings and gratitude lightened our load, opened our hearts and made our path clearer. The offerings, the prayers, the thanks given for the very breath we take in, are stepping-stones of oneness; every step deepens your experience, opening your heart to the universe. Offer your heart and give thanks to this entire sacred arising expression of the essence, the glory and the grace that is naturally present and always abiding. An offering is a prayer for this grace to continue guiding, confronting, and teaching us at every step. Make offerings to the wind rippling in the grass, prayers to the land, give thanks to the sky that you may open to the vast teachings before you, aligning your heart with the generosity of the intent of the essence.

OPENING YOUR HEART

In all these practices of letting go, there is a sense of stepping outside ordinary parameters and perceptions and becoming aware of a much wider view, a view that cannot be nailed down or defined in specific terms, it can only be felt and experienced in an allowing way. This is the realm of the heart. Original peoples naturally locate knowing in their hearts, as in the eloquent hand gesture sweeping out from the heart to indicate understanding in Native American sign language. Many peoples have recognized the heart as the center of true knowing. Relying on the wisdom of your heart is to accept the indwelling heritage of natural connection with the heart of all being.

REALM OF THE HEART

The heart quality is unbounded, outside judgments or comparisons and is not separate from the vision we call this life. Your heart knows how to respond to the expansiveness of the blue sky because we are all one within this vision; we are part of it, an integral love. The oneness that is here now all around us is felt directly in the heart. The energy of the heart is like water, it connects, there is no separation. In any body of water, whether river, pond, lake, or ocean, each molecule of water is joined to every other molecule of water so that they are essentially one molecule. And like water, the seamless fluidity of the heart is extremely responsive. Feelings radiating out from each being touch all other beings, they have an effect. A great deal of stress in contemporary human social interaction is due to the effort of denying our feelings or the feelings we are receiving from others. But feelings are valuable. Love, compassion, appreciation, and gratitude are the true actions of the heart. These feelings are the avenues to the expansive knowing that encompasses more than words and concepts. Gratitude to every aspect of this great arising vision opens your heart. Your heart opening is gratitude; they are one. The heart is not neutral; it is engaged. True caring, true love, true gratitude are powerful forces, they can move worlds, they can move you to fruition.

Some people have shadowed places in their hearts, something that happened in the past, either in childhood or in adulthood, a hurt. For some it is lodged in the heart as a black spot, a pain or a numbness, and they shy away from it. The simplest most effective way to move directly past those places and access the natural expansiveness of the heart is to go sit on the Earth on a good spot, a heart place. As you sit, you can also focus on breathing in and out through your heart for a few moments or longer, and then bring up strong feelings of love or appreciation. The effectiveness comes from being in your heart with the Earth, not visualizing or imagining but really feeling centered in your heart, really feeling love, really feeling appreciation. The breathing is a support and a way in; the love and appreciation and your relationship with the Earth are essential. You can do this as a practice; it will melt through the pain. Gradually you will be able to sustain the feelings of love and send them out to others, expanding your sphere of loving, merging with the nurturing energy of the Earth encompassing all beings, all life.

REALM OF THE INTELLECT

In our contemporary world, a vast majority of people are lost in opaque linear mind, the intellect afflicted by and enamored of its elaborations and certainties, separated from the heart. There are also many people doing spiritual practice who have been practicing for years and years and who have not let go of the world that has been created by this mind.

The opaque mind of the intellect is dense, insular, self-seduced; it cannot see outside its own view. It remains trapped in a hall of mirrors, ensnared in its own complexities and disconnected from direct perception, taking its interpretations of experience to be real. This reaches an apex in the philosophies in which all experience is held to be only a projection of the mind, a further expression of its self-absorption, but even without a formal philosophical stance, opaque mind is lost in itself within the fantasy it considers reality. Intellect has created a worldview that sees only itself, judging everything by its own criteria and discounting anything that does not fit, resulting in our contemporary mind so lost in its elaborations that it has forgotten its ability to listen to the heart. The intellect should be a support for the heart wisdom expressing itself. Instead, the intellect has gone beyond its natural function. It has taken over and become virulent, a parasite that no longer cares if it kills its host.

As agrarian cultures became increasingly separated from the natural rhythms of life, the mind divided the natural flow of being into sacred and profane. Spiritual experience became enshrined in special structures that mimicked the qualities of the natural world. The instinctive demand in the hearts of mystics throughout time to go deeper into the wilderness to make a direct connection with the indwelling sacredness of all life was exploited and relegated to temples consecrated not as part of the seamless continuity of life but as something other, a construct of the natural world.

Special places separate from nature but intended to reflect the spiritual experience, the soaring shapes of cathedrals, temples, and mosques evoked the presence of great trees in the forest and the vault of the sky, and later stained glass windows mimicked the inner radiance of rainbow light. Many religious structures are molded out of trees and stones into imitations of the vision that is this life, taken from what naturally arises and used for another purpose. They reinforce the idea that doctrine and authority are superior to direct experience in the wilderness. The natural world became suspect, something to be controlled and kept at bay. The vision that is this life now profane became something alien and dangerous.

The rise of agriculture had far-reaching repercussions on how we perceive our world and ourselves. Natural movement within cyclical time became linear history, life imprisoned in a line, now held between two points, poised always between here and there, before and after. We lost the inclusive encompassing dimensions of the eternal present and the heart. Instead of moving through time and space with the wide-angle view of the heart, open to subtle ever-changing shifts in the environment all around us, we began to attempt to own and control our world, clearing land and cultivating certain plants, often set in rows. We channeled the natural life of the waters, exiled plants that would not or did not serve our needs.

No longer moving within grace and change, we sought fixed conditions in soil, in crops and water supplies, and in our own minds. Religions arose that offered certainties and magic powers. Spiritual experience, no longer a matter of openness and clear perception of direct experience, was eclipsed by a need to impose patterns, subsumed in rituals to support our efforts to control and reshape our world. We sought structure and stability and became suspicious of fluidity and change. Rows and rows of identical crops required identical circumstances to be repeated reliably with no alien weeds. Rains had to come at the right time, but not too much and never during harvest. Tunnel mind arose with early cultivation through a need to focus, repeat, and impose a specific pattern of one-way interaction on a naturally fluid molten generously interactive world. Rhythms informing life were no longer those of acceptance of grace, of openness to the unexpected, but those of exclusion and demand. We isolated ourselves from life and in so doing, we isolated ourselves from the natural rhythms of our hearts and their resonate fields.

Rather than living and moving within a sacredness of manifest essence, we became petty gods, rulers over our own small plots carved out of a generous all. Ownership, hierarchy, status, and doctrine, calibrating with the mind, the intellect, replaced feeling from the heart and its wider scope of nuance. We have been drugged by the magic spell of the power of the intellect for so long that we take it to be human nature when in fact it is not. There are many ways to perceive and communicate outside the neural pathways of the brain. Electromagnetic energies move efficiently and swiftly throughout the galaxies, measurable in the background radiation of the universe, the signature of the cyclic nature of the cosmos, and in the heartbeat of the tiniest insect. The heart is the most powerful generator of electromagnetic energy in our bodies, producing far more electromagnetic energy than the brain. The brain will naturally follow the heart if we are centered in the heart instead of in our heads, and there are ways to become aware again from the natural seat of our souls, to heal and restore the original relationship of mind and heart.

Ironically, at this time on the Earth, as natural resources are being depleted or destroyed at an accelerating rate, one of the ways to heal is to grow a garden. Planting and tending a garden now offers a way to bridge the widening gap between our lives and the heart of the Earth. Gardening with respectful openness to the natural processes and cycles of plants and soil, as in Masanobu Fukuoka's way of natural farming, can connect us in a very direct way with the generosity and wisdom of the Earth and help us resanctify our most basic relationship with life. Gardening as a reciprocal act of cooperation can help heal the severance between daily and spiritual life, and support a path of freeing the heart from the cultivation of the mind.

HEARTFULNESS AND MINDFULNESS

In a culture dominated by the intellect, setting your mind to watch or investigate itself can be tricky. The mind is an obstacle when you let it lead, when you let it focus on itself. Your heart is the seat of compassion, joy, and light. This is where you want to experience life from; this is the true vantage point, the true view.

The heart is the natural seat of spiritual life. The practices of the heart involve a natural openness with qualities of a blended relationship that is nurturing and whole. Heartfulness is not the same process as using your mind to watch itself or to watch you do something. To go through a day of mindfulness checking and rechecking your practice, keeping careful account from the place of the mind, shuts down your connection with your heart. This leads to an intellectual idea or concept of spiritual progress that is a creation of the mind, a built structure of openness, the vault of a cathedral rather than the sky.

Heartfulness is a different process, a process of letting go into openness. All you must do is surrender to your heart, at all times. Heartfulness is a way of allowing the heart to be the basis of your experience of life. The Earth is all heart, and so going into a wilderness or any natural environment is extremely helpful. Being in wide-angle vision and Earth walking also bring you to your heart naturally without the burden of concepts, ideas, and doctrine, through blending your heart with the heart of the Earth and all that manifests out of essence. The intent of the essence is the heart; go to your heart as a way of being, not as a concept. Blend with the vision that is this life and become a part of the heartfulness of all being.

HEART AND MIND

For authentic living and spiritual growth, it is essential to know the difference between heart and mind in your own experience. In our present world order, so many of us are brought up and educated in a way that creates the common error of thinking our feeling, our knowing, and our spiritual practice. Many have become so indoctrinated, so habituated to this mode that they have no genuine experience, awareness, or memory of any other mode. Too often, sadness and grief are the only doorways left for feeling and they are often denied or repressed. Sadness or grief can be powerful openings to allow another way of experiencing to arise. They offer a gap that allows a new form of perception to flower, although many people shy away from the pain. This distancing upon distancing has led to the many horrible problems and disturbing events in our world that further reinforce the reflex to close down emotionally and view the world by remote through intellectualization. It is important to be able to distinguish between creations of the intellect and direct experience of the heart.

The heart speaks through images that arise organically inseparable with feelings and a wordless knowing. This becomes clearer the more you embrace the Earth within your own heart. The intellect uses words and can visualize but its images are different, crystalline in quality and constructed of details based on concepts and ideas of value and ranking rather than intuitive feeling. You need to recognize the difference between the labels, concepts, and judgments of the mind and the more open, inclusive, embraced perceptions of your heart as they speak to you. In whatever you do, you must be aware of the mind from the heart's perspective and see how the mind can hold and grasp on to anything, creating barriers instead of openings. Pay attention to what your feelings and your senses are telling you outside of words. We need to reenter our hearts and begin feeling again, no matter how painful at first, and reclaim direct experience and response. Outside the ordinary ways of perceiving that stifle this quality of heart, you enter the space of generous knowing that is oceanic yet simple, vast yet personal. You begin to perceive an openness that has no boundaries, a natural knowing, a receptive humble embrace as one touches, communicates with, and is taught by the manifest essence in all its myriad forms, from the cells in your body, dewdrops in the grass, the touch of a hand, the sounding of the stars in the night sky. True openness is reciprocal. You are not alone, you live within a dynamic interactive feeling universe, a dance of perceptions that meet and interact with the countless other perceptions of countless other lives. Your mind may be alone in its world of projections, but you are not. You are woven as one strand of light within the fabric of all life.

COURAGE

Now more than ever it takes great courage to live clearly and directly from the heart. The mind has gone unchallenged and has become increasingly authoritarian as it has extended its reach, and it has even taken for itself and intellectualized positive qualities that are the province of the heart. The basis of a spiritual life blended with manifest essence is the heart and the heart is courage. The word courage comes from the Latin root *cor*, meaning heart. The natural way to express our lives is to know the heart blended with the heart of all manifestation outside concepts and doctrine. This is a knowing that is a tone from origin, the source. It is felt in the heart, as the heart, and here lies courage, the courage to live a heart's path in the face of a pervasive view that endlessly promotes the perspective of the mind, a worldview that is destroying the heart of this Earth. Even without the elaborations and interferences of the mind, life naturally offers the full range of possible experience. The challenge is to stay with the openness of the heart, stay with the seat of courage. Courage is the heart, your connection with all life. Your relationship with your mind is not just a private affair; it affects all life around you. The courage to stand up to the dominance of the mind is on behalf of all being, it is honoring the heart of all.

THE INTENT WITHIN YOUR HEART

Following your heart is not following your ordinary desires; it is based on recognition of the luminous indwelling intent that naturally extends from your heart and encompasses all beings, all manifest aspects of this great vision. It is a reflection of the intent of the essence that all may experience this oneness and follow its light safely to fruition. This intent makes itself known not through contemplations of openness and compassion, but from actual experience of an open heart; you enter what you already are, touching it, feeling it with a passion outside of thought, a love beyond desire, and a surrender without loss.

The intent of the essence within this entire unfolding vision is that all beings return, that they recognize their own true nature and follow the path back home. Openness as a natural knowing is an aspect of this larger intent. It arises as a feeling, a force within your heart, not as a cognitive expression of a purpose, but more like a wordless prayer, a concentric ring expanding outward. This reflection of the larger intent will propel you forward along the path. It is an actual energy, like the life in a seed bursting forth, pushing up from the root through the soil to reach the light. This natural intent is not separate from the essence. It has the strength and resolve of a mountain and the fluidity and expansiveness of the ocean, and it moves you toward resolution, the truth that you already are, felt and experienced within your heart.

The intent within your heart is fluid, expansive, unbounded; it is not linear or narrow in scope. Its basis is oneness, and to meet this intent is to touch the initiating force behind it, the intent of the essence. An open heart connects you; you blend, you touch union, a purpose at the very core of all manifestation, so that essence may reflect back to itself in you and all beings. Anyone who truly opens his or her heart touches this expansive prayer, limitless, universal, a love outside of time.

THE CHOICE

The intent of the essence within this manifest world includes the ability to choose. We are here to learn spiritually, and there is a spiritual choice that everyone must make, a choice all the more critical now with the accelerating scope of the intellect. It is a choice of aligning your deepest resolve, your personal will, with your heart or aligning it with your mind. This is a pivotal choice; it determines the outcome of the path. The path of the heart brings you to the oneness of true resolution, a timeless merging beyond union and separation. The path of the mind will not bring you to this resolution of phenomena, will not bring you to your heart blended with the heart of essence. Instead, it can take you to power, elaboration, formalism, and holding to doctrine. You need to know why you are doing spiritual practice in the first place. Ask your heart; be very honest with yourself. How much are you using spiritual practice to fortify rather than dismantle personal identity and a sense of special self? How much are you using your practice to create a spiritual ego? To cultivate a practice that reinforces opaque mind or inflates self-identity clothed as spiritual insight and prowess will blind you and distort your perceptions. The intellect can make you think you are having spiritual experiences, and it can commandeer heart energies and shape them to its own purposes, creating simulated emotions based on comparisons and judgments that have nothing do with true heart values of love, compassion, and gratitude. The heart is the natural seat of your being, and when you cut through the entanglements of the intellect and reclaim the translucent inward power of your heart, you will naturally come to deeper experiences of openness, with more willingness to relate, and more love, compassion, and gratitude welling up spontaneously from your heart.

PERSEVERANCE AND SURRENDER

The art of spiritual practice is one of maintaining openness, of harnessing your resolve in a way that does not solidify a new sense of self-identity around perseverance on the path. Staying with openness in a way that is neither rigid nor forced and remains connected, not distanced, from whatever passes into the field of that openness is natural for the heart. For separate identity upheld by the mind, perseverance means to hold to your position, your stance, no matter what, and surrender is failure, loss. Yet from the heart's perspective, perseverance and surrender are one fluid whole, a movement of embrace, of opening freely, blending without fear, not using ideas of emptiness or illusion to dismiss the impact of whatever you meet, but meeting whole-heartedly just as it is, your openness enfolding and embracing rather than pulling back. The ability to remain open within the widening view of full engagement comes from the heart. For the heart there are no differences between perseverance and surrender, they are one essential act.

SURRENDERING TO YOUR HEART

Surrendering to your heart is a practice that is helpful for shifting your energy from being centered in the intellect to being centered in the heart. The first step is to bring yourself to a calm state, like water in a still pond. It is best to begin by lying down in a warm comfortable place. Later as you become more accustomed to this practice, you can go into the meditation in any posture, but at first, lie down on your back with your hands at your sides and your legs uncrossed. Take a few moments to settle in, then take a deep breath and hold it, tense all the muscles of your body all at once and then release them completely as you breathe out. You may want to tense different parts of your body sequentially, beginning at your feet, with a series of breaths. Eventually you will only need a single deep breath with a slight pause and a faint muscle tension to release and relax. Imagine that you are standing in a shower of vibrant white light. Feel the light pouring all around you and into the crown of your head and down through your body to your feet. This light begins to fill your body from your feet upward like bright living water filling a clear glass. Once your whole body is glowing, rest in that for a few gentle breaths. Take another deep breath, hold it briefly, and then let it all out, surrendering to your heart. This is a feeling outside of words, outside of knowing how; you give yourself completely to the energy of your heart. Feel the relaxed weight of your body sinking slowly toward the Earth. Then out of that sinking, melting feeling, you begin to float upward as the brightness that you are lifts up out of the weight. You can rest and refresh yourself in the floating brightness for a while, or you can continue into another meditation.

BODY OF LIGHT

A simple yet profound exercise for recognizing the radiant openness already within you is to move with it. First center yourself and surrender to your heart while standing. Then imagine your body made of rainbow light, translucent and shimmering, one step in front of you, facing in the same direction that you are facing. Any physical ailments that you may have are not there. Any self-limiting ideas or feelings of inadequacies are also absent. Then slowly step into the body of light, as if you were water pouring into a clear glass. Feel yourself becoming the perfection, shimmering with light and seeing through eyes of light. Remain standing and allow your body of light to slowly sit down right where you are, seeing clearly through its eyes as it descends, seeing the landscape change as your vantage point lowers. Once the body of light is sitting, take a moment to look around at the landscape through its eyes. As you remain focused in the view from the light body, slowly allow your physical body to sit down into it. Once your physical body is sitting within the body of light, turn them together to face another direction. Then the body of light slowly stands up while the physical body remains sitting. Again, pay attention to the view through your eyes of light as you rise. Once your body of light is standing, look around through its eyes, and then slowly allow your physical body to

73

stand up into the body of light. Continue sitting and standing a number of times. This can be a very effective way to shift your perceptions and recognize that you are not confined within your physical body or your ordinary states of mind and habits of identity. It is particularly effective when done outdoors; you can see details of the landscape through the eyes of your body of light that you may not have seen through your regular eyes.

DREAMING

The mind tends to compartmentalize, keeping outer and inner experience separate, but actual experience of the heart is interactive and inclusive. We share a natural fluidity of experience with all beings. As you recognize this permeable quality, subjective and objective lose their defining boundaries. You begin to erase the border between perception and participation in a dynamic communicative world. Dreams, signs, and visions become meaningful aspects of your life as you open your heart and respond, recognizing that you are already immersed in a vast ocean of experience in which nothing is separate and everything is alive.

Dreaming can provide another way to access perceptions outside the familiar limits of the physical senses. Personal and transcendent, shadow and light, past, present, and future, possible and impossible, all worlds intertwined, learning to orient yourself within this fluid sphere can help you greatly along the path. Dreaming offers an arena in which you can shift the habits of mind and its insistence on solidity, time, and space and can help you recognize the visionary quality of all your experience. There are many methods to engage this energy and numerous books have been written about techniques for dreaming. The basic choice is to intervene in the process or allow it to happen. You can cultivate lucid dreaming, becoming aware that you are dreaming within a dream by locating an object or scene that you have chosen and focused on before you go to sleep, but you run the risk of limiting the natural expansiveness of the dreaming state by the concerns of the mind. You can choose instead to be open to whatever the dreaming presents to you, respecting the dreams as clues to a more fluid knowing outside your normal waking mind. Very much like waiting for animals without expectation or manipulation, you open to another dimension of experience, a deeper level of dreaming through which the wholeness of your heart can also speak to you and share with you its ability to communicate spontaneously in a flowing natural way.

SIGNS

As you open to your heart, you become more aware of your heart's connection with the heart of all life. You begin to recognize the specific ways that the essence is communicating with you in waking life. Signs and omens arise as messages, expressions of the essence. But understanding and knowing how to interpret these signs involves a true listening in your heart, and it takes time to learn how to hear, see, feel, and touch these messages without embellishing or projecting. This comes from practice, from settling into our mother the Earth, and surrendering to your heart.

Synchronicities, natural phenomena, and the behavior of animals and insects may give warnings or clues, directions, and answers to choices you need to make, or indicate future events long before they happen. All manner of communications are possible within the living interrelationships of the shared vision we call this world. They may arise to startle you, shake you, or gently guide you, through events that are clearly outside the patterns of ordinary habitual life. Animals may act in ways that are uncharacteristic for them, with unusual behavior, or familiar behavior that is unusually close to you, or relating directly with you in some way as when a bird calls as it flies low over your head or a fox walks right up to you. When you begin to experience this deeper communication, be sensitive to the varying factors all around you at the moment of the sign: the time of day, position of the sun or moon, cardinal directions, and any other relational aspect that comes to the attention of your heart. Allow all of these aspects to paint a picture that you feel intuitively. Do not force it, but let the picture settle into your heart, and awareness and a knowing will arise within you.

VISION QUEST

The vision quest has been taught within many traditional cultures. It is an ancient way to open to your heart and experience a deeper communication with the essence that can guide you through the rest of your life. There are numerous ways to approach this sacred practice of time apart in the wilderness, which usually involves fasting from all food and in some traditions from water as well, and various preparations, ceremonies, and sequences of time. Rather than offer guidelines here, we would like to share some aspects of questing we have experienced that are relevant to blending your heart with the heart of essence.

When you take the first step into your quest circle, you have already prayed for guidance and given thanks to all life, all teachers. As you cross the threshold into a vision quest, you leave everything outside your circle, all prayers, all spiritual practice, and all the concerns and worries of your life. You enter into a sphere of simplicity, a time of openness. You place yourself within the embrace of manifest essence, and your only duty is to be open and aware, to see and hear with your heart the teachings that will be imparted to you about your life's path. You pay respectful attention to everything going on around you; the essence is speaking to you through the natural world, through animals, birds, and insects, plants and trees, the sun and moon, and also through the visionary avenue of your heart. It is truly a time held within the heart and basis of all experience. There is only openness and your ability to wait, waiting without filling up the space with anything else, waiting without waiting, settling within an undefined and open space. This experience leads you to an even deeper opening of your heart, for there is a fluid potency within this waiting, feeling the rhythms of the essence, which opens a visionary doorway.

There are many concepts about visionary experience, but the point is to come to your vision quest purely from your heart, with an openness to whatever may arise. Watch and feel everything that is presented to you, from a sunset to the tinniest insect or a soft breeze. Open with gratitude to all that speaks to you in the countless voices of the intent of essence, focusing, like the sun's rays through a single drop of water, all your intent and heart into a single circle of experience that opens beyond time.

HELL SIT

In a vision quest, you are opening to the essence, entering into resonance with its field, trusting and blending with a generosity far outside the scope of self. In a hell sit, you learn to trust the openness of your heart in the face of negative forces that are decidedly not generous, that are hostile and holding to separation. A hell sit is an experience of maintaining openness and love for all life in the face of fear. It breaks down barriers within yourself that have held you back and strengthens your commitment to the path and your resolve to reach fruition and bring benefit to all life.

This kind of experience not only brings you up against your own negativity, but also puts you in contact with negative forces that condense within the fabric of this world. Certain places hold the energy of harmful actions and emotions very strongly, and some areas actually have a negative force far older than human activity. Spirits are also attracted to these energies. They can be seen as dull lights or shadows and are as varied as all the degrees of emotions and energies that they are drawn to.

The single most important aspect of this practice is to know your purpose, the intent of your spiritual life. As you embark on the spiritual path, you want positive qualities and circumstances for yourself and others to increase. As your connection to the intent within your heart strengthens, you trust that connection, and your practice becomes a living prayer integrated with the intent of essence, a prayer for all life, a prayer that all beings, positive or negative, recognize and blend with the oneness of essence. This is a deep-seated love, a reflection of the very compassion that fostered you. It is this core love that can hold at bay all the demons throughout space. This intent is not a power to overcome, but a compassionate force, a cellular love, which enters the hearts of all beings, an intent beyond self, encompassing all.

Sitting with negative energies is best undertaken with the guidance of an experienced teacher who can place you on an appropriate spot for your spiritual growth. Then, alone, usually at night in an isolated place or woodland, in an environment that is negative but not outwardly dangerous, you abide with your purpose, confronting not only the negative forces around you but also the uncontrolled nature of your mind. This experience forces you to see how your mind on its own adds to the outward development of any experience. If your mind stands down and aligns itself with the natural openness of your heart, positive and expansive with an intention to benefit all life and the Earth, then the negative entities that come will pass you by. They may put you to the test, pushing you to your limits, but they will subside, their power weakened from the love pouring over them. But if your thoughts run away with fear, anger, or other negative emotions and feelings, the entities will grow in strength. They will harass you, overtake your mind, or even bring about your death. Through the hell sit, you can come to a genuine confidence in the power of spiritual practice as you experience directly the depth of the intent within your heart and the fading of negative forces. You also come to a more expansive view of the negative forces themselves, seeing them as teachers. The truth of this life is that the radiance of the essence pushes and pulls us in myriad ways to guide and teach.

THE CHARNEL GROUND

The charnel ground encompasses a much larger dynamic than a hell sit in a fearful place. The cremation grounds of ancient India were set apart on the outskirts of cities and were revered by spiritual practitioners of many different paths. Amid rotting corpses, scattered bones, roving spirits, and the stench of decay, practitioners also found wildflowers, songbirds, open sky, and forests of fragrant trees. They found a natural freedom in places uncultivated, unrestrained, and intense, with danger, death, and a wild beauty both delicate and raw, seldom frequented except by those seeking to go beyond, seeking to go outside, to break all attachments of the mind. The charnel ground is the interface of true wilderness and the structures of culture, the meeting ground of the known, the unknown, and the unknowable. It is a place of letting go, the place of death, the corpse, the forces of decay, a gap that allows the dissolution of your opaque, acculturated mind, a place of transition and transformation, a place of dissolution and resolution.

The charnel ground is another aspect of the sacred intent in your heart. This intent takes you out of your ordinary concepts and perceptions; it forces you, confronts you, demands that you see everything as it is, the good and the bad. You are compelled to go to places that will move you, challenge you, and shift your perceptions utterly, and coupled with a deep desire to benefit all life, this will propel you forcefully along your path. Like true renunciation, the charnel ground is not so much cultivated as it is honored when it arises, but like waiting for animals, you can watch and be ready for it, and accept its presence in your life with a grateful heart.

As your willingness to let go beyond yourself gains strength and momentum and your intent enlarges in scope, you may find yourself changing significant aspects of your life. This may be a natural outgrowth of your progress in changing habits of identity or perception, or it may be a parallel process already in motion ripening at its own pace and in its own way, as it did for us. The pattern of renunciation developing over many lives may be awakening on its own. Careers, family, friends, home, land, financial security, jobs, achievements, major categories of hard-won identity, you may find yourself shedding them unexpectedly. Fragile, brittle, tissue-thin, they slough off easily; you cannot hold them if you try. You find yourself strangely vulnerable and free at the same time, open in what will perhaps seem to others a precarious way, and perilous. You have accomplished an important and difficult aspect of the path; you have reached the charnel ground within yourself.

The charnel ground can arise in many ways, in any life, in any culture or time. We found our charnel ground in outer landscapes, urban and wilderness, and in the choices we made to totally alter our way of life: moving to new areas, changing the way we lived and worked, and how we defined ourselves. This was an organic expression of our spiritual lives as we began to see through the overlay of ordinary identities. The charnel ground is a movement within your whole being, a force driving you to leave your familiar world and enter the wilderness, the unknown. If you are compelled from your deepest heart to enter the charnel ground, you enter a freedom to see and learn beyond ordinary constructs. You realize a crucial, vital space within you, an opening for new energy to move upward and unmask the essence that you already are.

THE SPIRITUAL PATH

In ancient times when a man or a woman felt within their hearts a burning desire and need to follow the spiritual path beyond rhetoric, these ancients had to leave all that they knew and loved to find a blended experience with essence in the wilderness far away from the holding patterns of society. The people who left and began to wander, searching for the teacher calling in their hearts, had reached an important stage on the path, an important decision. They may have known how to find water, shelter, and food, but this journey could take months or years, and these ancient followers of the heart had to have great courage to take the first step. In this experience, the student already had an open heart and knew how to follow this timeless call. They knew how to listen and find the call within their direct experience.

THE ROLE OF THE GUIDE

The role of the guide is to be a doorway to your own direct experience of the radiance of the intent of essence. The ultimate guide is the essence. Manifest essence as nature is the guidance, always there if you are truly open, the basis of spiritual life and visionary experience. An animal, a plant, mountains, rivers, the soil under your feet can teach beyond words the lessons of the universe. They are the voice of the essence, a natural call of return sounding within your heart, personal, direct, spiritual life as vision.

A human guide can show you aspects that you may have missed and push, pull, prod, or lead you in directions you may not have seen, but a true guide also knows that he or she is only a pointer for the next generation to experience the patterns of fruition already woven within this manifest world. A guide is also humble in the act of initiating a change in the student. Guides know they are only helping others toward their own direct experience of the intent of essence. They are one within the vision that is this life, and once they have offered their vision to the essence and the next generation, they will pass from this life. They care nothing for titles, lineage, or other external authorization through some cultural framework. They are a simple, humble part of this manifest realm.

A human guide has accomplished the whole path, the resolution of phenomena. For them, nothing less is acceptable. He or she is now here for all life, not just humans. He or she is a constant ripple of concentric rings, fluid and soft, stretching out upon a pond's surface. Most people would not notice a true guide; most are seeking attributes of concepts associated with power. The true guide is unencumbered by concepts and will be like a weathered stone along a path, easily missed by those whose eyes are dazzled by hopes of power, fame, and grandeur. The true guide is here for those who have an open heart and the courage and perseverance to overcome the limiting concepts that maintain the personal container of self. The guidance is simple yet profound, a gesture toward direct experience of those whom he or she is guiding. The important part of guiding is to help them reach fruition, to see the vision that is this life through the eyes of the vision itself, the eyes of inner radiance. The guide is a natural part of this manifest world and those who seek a guide are just as simple. They have no other desire but a movement in their heart, a courage to experience essence as essence, as a dewdrop falls upon the surface of the pond.

The true guides in nature, vision, or in human form, are manifest essence naturally so, unencumbered by culture or doctrine; they are one with all that manifests within the vision that is this life. The goal, the fruition, is not just another concept. The stone weathering along the path is one with all life; he or she is within all experience, happy or sad, open to the feelings within the currents of their times yet still the stone that weathers, beingness embedded as vision in vision. The goal is not happiness, power, or joy; it is beingness as the heart of all life.

WILLINGNESS TO CHANGE

Unlike spiritual seekers in early times who could leave their familiar world, followers of the heart in our contemporary world have fewer options to leave society and go into the wilderness to follow a spiritual path. Social structures are becoming increasingly complex, and it is also harder now to release yourself from the internalized mental complexity in which we live. Yet luminous awareness and awakened heart are natural and unelaborate and require simple means to actualize them. The challenge now is all the greater because the contemporary worldview is so omnipresent, and it is difficult to touch the unelaborate truth while still enmeshed in complex patterns. To break through requires a courage that comes from aligning your deepest intent with your heart, with your love.

Most people experience their lives through the expectations and conditions given to them by others, which are then upheld by their own minds. Fear of stepping outside the safety zone, outside convention, presents a big problem on the spiritual path. Spiritual practice can unfortunately tap the desire for safety and demand a secure orthodox universe where nothing can disturb the assumed order. Many children, particularly in early childhood, are naturally open to spiritual experience outside doctrine. Adults around them often steer them toward the safety zone, but the quality of open heart that is so present in early childhood is still within the hearts of adults, waiting to be embraced again.

The most precious aspect of human birth is the ability and willingness to choose and to change. This is the basis of creativity. True creativity is not necessarily about art: it is about opening to possibilities within this manifest vision and being willing to try, to explore, and even to fail. The creative process naturally allows opposites to coexist without holding to either side and can embrace the energy moving between them. Not holding to one form allows a dynamic wholeness to emerge, moving in harmony with the fluidity of this manifest vision. Spiritual practice is an art, not in the sense of making drawings, or paintings, or music, but in the sense of being able to move within and be open to experience outside your boundaries, to be open to grace, to allow yourself into the flow of the ineffable.

The spiritual path will change you. If you have an idea that you can do spiritual practice and keep your ordinary life intact, you are mistaken and your mind has control over your heart. You will change; your life will not be one of structure, of holding to preconceived concepts of normal life. You enter a river that flows to the sea, fluid, not linear, a path of heart toward a blended embrace.

FEAR

The biggest obstacle to being willing to change is fear. As you move along the spiritual path you naturally encounter fear in many forms, not only fears associated with danger or death, but also fears associated with the spiritual path itself: fear of confronting the shadow side of your mind, your experiences, memories, and habitual tendencies from past lives; fear of letting go of your familiar, smaller self; fear of the naturally fluid, ephemeral nature of experience, the lack of inherent solidity of the structures of this or any life, fear that there is nothing there; fear of the world of spirits, fear of the entities that are moving around us all the time; or fear of the true radiance and joy of light, a brilliance that can be overwhelming in its splendor.

Whatever fear arises, in whatever situation it comes up for you, the only way to deal with it is to just keep going, keep practicing. You do not deny your fear; you still act appropriately in relation to the dangers of this world. You have an intent to follow a spiritual life, and you do your best to stay alive to see it through. You do not run from your fear or let it stop you from learning on the path, but you can be skillful in how you engage with it. If you find that you are sitting on a bad spot and it is bringing up a heavy fear that honestly seems beyond your ability to deal with at that time, you may want to move to another area with the intention to set up good circumstances to strengthen your resolve to deal with it in the future. Being honest with your self is crucial. Some people have already given into fear but they are not aware that they have conceded to it. They may not feel afraid, but they stop learning, and they back away from spiritual growth, from the challenges of letting go. Someone who has lost to fear has closed his or her mind. They may be either timid or intimidating in their behavior, but people who have lost to fear want to keep their attachments; they do not want to let go anymore. The gift of life is here for us to do the best we can to learn and grow. You have to take a chance, you may even get hurt along the way, but the courage to move beyond fear is within your heart and the heart of every being.

MEDITATIVE EXPERIENCE

Once you have embarked on a spiritual path, and you are willing to open to deepening levels of experience, you will encounter a number of meditative states that are common to many spiritual traditions. Bliss, clarity, and non-thought arise naturally in varying degrees, and it is important to be aware of them so you do not become caught up in them and are able to move with them and through them without holding. None of these experiences are wrong or harmful; they are actually signs of progress. But as they arise, they seem so fresh and wonderful, so different from how your practice has been before, that you can become very attached to these meditative states. The key to the path is to let go and not hold to anything, letting your heart be open, allowing whatever arises to come and go. Bliss, clarity, and non-thought can arise throughout your spiritual life, so you need to learn to ride these experiences without grasping onto them.

Bliss is one of the most compelling meditative experiences, and it can be difficult to let go of this energetic level of spiritual growth. Bliss is part of the rise of energy moving up the central channel to the crown chakra, and it brings a feeling of great joy, an ecstatic state that can be almost orgasmic. This feeling can help open and energize you during long meditative retreats. The problem comes when practitioners seek and hold to bliss. You need to allow bliss to arise and fade naturally without clinging, recognizing that it is a sign of the natural fluidity of experience flowing like an endless stream.

Clarity is a kind of confidence that you touch as your practice becomes less confused. It is a sense of a clear knowing, a feeling about the path, your practice, and your life that was not there before. The experience of clarity can be dramatic in comparison to your previous meditative states, but you need to realize that it is only a sign, a way to know that you are on the right path. If you hold to it at this stage, you think you are becoming stable. True stability is much deeper, so just keep going, no matter how clear and lucid your experience becomes.

Non-thought also arises naturally throughout your spiritual life in varying degrees, from an initial occasional fading of your thoughts to the dissolving of concepts farther along the path. In some traditions non-thought is a goal, but it is still an aspect of the expression of the essence; it is not the pure, resolved experience of essence itself. There is a more fundamental awareness underlying non-thought. Again, it is important to not be attached to these states or make one experience better than another. The experience of non-thought is a sign of progress, a quality of the expressed essence moving through you, but you do not hold to it.

CERTAINTY

After you have been practicing for some time and know how to let go, you will come to experience a deeper kind of clarity, a sense of accomplishment and understanding, the finger in the light socket, aha! I've got it stage. You think that you have really gotten somewhere; you feel a seductive confidence. This is just another stage. It may seem wonderful, but you have to let it go. If you succumb to certainty, you will become overconfident. You will think you know, it will blind you, and you will make the mistake of assuming that you have already accomplished the path before you have gone very far. You may become reckless and squander your spiritual energy.

At every stage of the spiritual path, you will encounter degrees of both certainty and uncertainty. Uncertainty is by far the best support. The core of the practice and all experiences of the heart are outside definition, outside the borders that maintain certainties, and so you want to cultivate a way of being that is uncertain, flexible, fluid, and humble.

POWER

Power can be a natural outgrowth of the spiritual path. It arises for each practitioner in different ways, at different stages of their development. Some people are born with special abilities, some are fascinated with acquiring powers, and others give them little thought for they are more focused on completing the entire path. Power is not synonymous with spiritual realization. Some highly realized practitioners do not exhibit powers. Some practitioners who manifest extraordinary powers have little or no realization. Flying through the sky, going through walls, knowing all things, can all come from lesser forms of practice. Power in and of itself is not a defining aspect of resolving all phenomena and abiding in genuine being blended within essence. Whenever clairvoyance or other forms of powers begin to arise, they can be an expression of your spiritual growth, but they are not realization, do not hold to them. Let them come and go, or you will fall to this challenge of the spiritual path. Power gives you a sense that you can manipulate, and even though you may have good purpose or intent, you can get lost in this kind of mastery. Power can ensnare you, and you want to control more and more. You lose your openness, dominate situations and others, and if you are not vigilant, you can stray into high-minded cruelty. Power is not really yours; it is an expression of the essence, temporarily moving through you. You really need to stay with your heart, with the recognition that you are a part of the essence moving through all life, honoring this connection with true humbleness, knowing that you still have a long way to go on the path.

CONCEPTS OF ENLIGHTENMENT

We would like to speak here about a very special spiritual challenge that each practitioner comes to decisively at some point along their path, the challenge to accept that awakened heart is naturally abiding within you and that you are allowed to actualize it and that you can. Fruition is not only for people of another time or another culture, or for super heroes who live in celestial realms far way; it is not outside you. Buddhahood, fruition, enlightenment, liberation, realization, are all grand expressions for what is already indwelling in your heart. Awakened heart is vast in scope; it has nothing to do with the mind or the attributes that mind projects on it, often as inflated versions of itself. All concepts are impediments and some concepts ensnare us more than others. Even ideas or concepts that inspire you at first can hold you back. You need to go beyond the labels and trust your heart; your heart is already your connection to awakening. It is your connection to the source of the call and the courage to follow it. Awakened heart is an indwelling heritage that all beings share. Fruition is a natural organic process woven into every aspect of this naturally arising vision. The experience of awakened heart is outside culture and language, beyond self, beyond concepts of solidity, time, and space. It is outside the ideas that the mind ascribes to it. But expressions of awakened heart are all around us, in the fluidity of water, the openness of the sky, the patient generosity the of Earth. These are but a few of the abundant qualities of awakened heart within this manifest world. You can touch them and experience them within your own heart now, outside of words.

NATURE

All followers of the heart, all mystics of any tradition have a deep heart connection with nature. It is a natural outgrowth of spiritual practice that one is drawn into the intent of essence through the dynamic beauty and joy of nature. The vision that is this life is manifest essence, the intent arising as the natural world in all its variety of place and form to guide all beings to the embrace of essence. But even in the early stages of spiritual growth you can experience this world as a fluid dance of direct experience. Every moment, every movement within the vision that is this life is alive with sign, dream, and vision. We are already blended into and within this shared vision; let go and slowly slip into the flow of nature to recognize the indwelling heart of all experience.

The blending of your heart with nature is a good sign. All mystics, all original spirits of the heart, know the natural world is the home, the temple, and the shrine. If you find yourself turning toward structure and doctrine, it is a sign that your mind has control over your heart and your spiritual practice. Only when you blend with the vision that is this life can you know you are going in the right direction.

The call to go into the wilderness as part of your spiritual growth is ageless and nearly universal. Even people in cultures that already live within the natural world seek time apart in wilderness to deepen their connection with the source of all. It is natural to seek solitude apart from the constructs of human society of any kind to hear the voice of all life woven from the single voice of the source, to find your spiritual home in the wilderness.

ILLUMINATION

The pace of spiritual growth is different for everyone, and there are many different maps for the path already laid out in your heart by the intent of essence, but there are some stages of spiritual transformation that are intrinsic to many paths.

For many, engagement with the path of the heart begins with an initiatory experience of illumination, a personal encounter with radiance. Illumination is extremely compelling. It can come to you in many ways, whether in dream, vision, near death experience, or a shocking event in your life, and it may be of varying degrees of intensity, from an initial glimpse of indwelling brilliance like the glint of light on water to a full-blown experience of inner radiance. Illumination has a tone similar to clarity and certainty, but clarity and certainty are colored by the mind, while illumination has the flavor of touching and being touched directly in your heart, a relating with and within a living brilliance. It is an opening, a connection, a relationship. The illumination can be glorious and brings with it a sense of meeting and being met by something luminous beyond self, which can lead to a sense of accomplishment and knowing when the mind grabs onto this experience, but this is only a stage. In whatever form it comes into your life, and it may arise a number of times, know that it is a sign, a guidance toward a true embrace. It is important that you do not become caught up in the experience, suspended on the path, blinded by your own headlights.

Many people have had experiences of the illumination and have become overwhelmed by them, leaving their path and going out to teach and elucidate on the incredible experience they have had, and in all this, they lose their energy and resolve to continue. They become stuck in the afterglow. They may seem bright, joyful, and confident, but illumination is only a portal that you must enter and then pass through. The illumination is one of the first major acknowledgements of the intent of essence, a taste, a touch, a sometimes not so gentle, brilliant slap in the face. The illumination, though glorious and wonderful, and so compelling that you want everyone to know about it, is fundamentally a personal experience, and when disentangled from the mind's attempts to co opt and exploit it, becomes a secret memory, a longing in your heart, a yearning to be touched again by its grace in every new experience. It is a reflection of the source and a marker for the direction of return to essence.

THE NIGHT

The night is a spiritual night, a silence of light where the glow from the illumination dies to nothing and you are left on the path seemingly in the dark. It is sometimes referred to as the dark night of the soul but the experience of the night does not need to hold the dread that this phrase can engender. The night brings an inward turning, a quietness that pervades your spiritual path. You may feel that nothing speaks to you and that grace has left you. You are left alone on the path, waiting with an unknowing knowing, a simple trust. Grace has not gone away; it is speaking to you with a different voice and in the silence of this night, you are learning to listen and surrender from a deeper level of your heart.

The angst quality of this stage of the path only arises if you are not letting go, if you are holding with your mind to an experience of illumination and resisting the changes that are already coming to you. Within the loss of the illumination, you learn to listen in the dark silence to something new. Staying with your heart no matter what you are feeling keeps you in touch with grace. This is a powerful time. You are learning to listen beyond words, trust beyond trust, see beyond light. You are shifting your center of gravity to another dimension of experience.

CROSSING THE PASS

As you continue to progress along the heart's path, eventually after years of concerted practice you will come to the stage at which your recognition of the indwelling luminous awareness of your heart becomes an ongoing experience, no longer moments of awareness brightening the path and then dying away to be again recalled. The glimpse that you had during the illumination stage of an open engaged radiance has been allowed to arise from your heart again and again within the immediacy of your direct experience. Recognized without holding and grasping, it has become a part of your life. You have crossed an important threshold. Now luminous awareness never leaves; the clouds of one's mind are no longer obscuring the breath of essence in your heart and pervading all existence. This is an ongoing state, a natural organic connection with the underlying foundation of the vision that is this life, not just a quality of perception; it is the fabric of being. Most people do not get this far; many become stuck within their minds, thinking and simulating the stages of the path. Crossing the pass is a gentle glory and a great happiness that arises from the sky of your heart like the dawn in early spring, touching all life.

THE EMBRACE

Within the embrace, there are no more stages; there is no further path. It is an experience of total and complete resolution of all being, your sphere of influence blended effortlessly into essence, like water into water, a seamless oneness.

The culmination of the spiritual path has many words and concepts associated with it. Doctrine and even politics have worked their way into belief systems of the final passage. Following the motion of a circle, the completion is inherent in the path from the beginning. The path comes around to meet itself, a time of decline and resolution, a time of passage into a new life. This is a natural cycle, a movement within all cycles of the universe. The final path is the same, the culmination of letting go into a relationship with the intent of essence, moving in the flow of a stream that is beyond primordial. You allow your heart to guide you within an utter embrace. This is not the domain of the mind, but a true engagement with the intent within and beyond all that naturally manifests.

At the time of the embrace, luminous awareness has been stable for quite a while, free of the constraints of the mind; the world of experience has revealed itself in its manifest form as rainbow light, and essence becomes apparent, the blue-black depth of all. It is just a moment and a step away from complete union, essence into essence.

All that is left is just a shell that becomes less and less as the essence within begins to blend with essence beyond manifestation, never separate from total and complete union. This is a visceral experience involving all being, a resolution of all that manifests as a seamless whole. Stability in luminous awareness alone does not bring you to this culmination. This resolution of all your being and the world around you, this resolving of the radiance, is the completion of Tögal. The path of the light of intent found in your heart does not belong to any group or tradition; the light is its own passage to resolution, free, unowned by any structure. You lay aside all that manifests, all that has guided you up to this point, now a sphere of influence blended in essence, nothing not nothing, a potential ringing with intent, a true embrace.

DECLINE

Whether you have reached the resolution in this life or not, you will face the natural process of decline one way or another. If you have not completed the path before old age envelopes you, you run the risk of giving in to tiredness and other basic afflictions of old age that can sap your energy and your resolve to persevere. You can become fixated on eternal life or on other forms of salvation elsewhere in heavenly or pure realms. The last part of the practice, the last part of the path, may well be the hardest even without old age, and you will need all your strength and openness fully engaged here, now.

The decline is a natural movement of turning inward. It can be a turning inward of personal self toward childhood memories, or a turning inward of the wider scope of the embrace. If you have given into fear, illumination, or power, you will turn the more constricted scope of those energies inward. You do not escape the inward turning; however far you have gotten along the path when you reach the decline, you turn the summation of that experience inward to set the seed of the next life.

In linear expansionist cultures, there is a widespread fear of the cyclical aspects of life and experience, and especially a fear of the natural cycle of decline. The desire for eternal youth and powers to fight off or deny the decline into death comes from not understanding the self-surrender of setting seed, and can be an obstacle at this stage of life.

Depending on the pattern of your life, the decline can come at any time. You begin to see that your life is cresting, turning toward the dissolution. If your life path allows, you will grow into old age, but you can also face a critical illness or sudden death at any age, and in those cases, the decline will be drastically compressed. As your life energies begin to crest, you must look into your heart and see the life around you and your responsibility to it; this time is crucial. You must complete your path as far as it will take you, in whatever time your path allows.

If you reach the time of old age, it does not necessarily mean a time of rest. It can be a time of greater determination rooted in the warm joy in your heart, knowing your responsibility to all life and in every step you take expressing the joy that flows from the heart of intent within all that manifests. Many physical problems can arise in old age but your heart knows that you are needed. You may not move with the grace that you once had but still there is a way for you to act and share your heart with others. This is a time of setting the seed for your next life and for the lives of those around you, focusing on the most essential life-engendering aspects of your experience. If you are a person of heart then the time of final decline into death is not a sad one; it is just another path, for you are always moving in the flow of intent like a ring of light moving farther and farther out on a pond's surface, always blended in brilliance.

ORIGINAL HEART
ORIGINAL NATURE

Within this great manifest vision are all the clues we need for the path of return to essence. Sit quietly in a light rain beside a small pond or at the shallow edge of a river and watch as the drops of rain create rings of movement on the water, concentric circles expanding outward, overlapping and interacting with other circles. Sometimes the rain will also make fragile spheres, bubbles that float on the surface, some touching other bubbles, some alone, all seemingly stable until they pop. In the same way, all phenomena are spheres of being emanating from the essence.

Inner experience of the all-pervasive essence is found within our personal sphere of being. The recognition involves a subtle shift: you see the contrast between the confined yet ephemeral aspects of the mind and the true sky of your heart, an embrace of all being, an openness, natural, and abiding. Within this expansive sky-like experience, there is a sense of knowing, a knowing outside of any conceptualization, an open embrace that has no boundaries, edges or restrictions of any kind. This is luminous awareness, none other than the recognized nature of essence reflecting out of your heart and all manifestation. Our eyes, the globe of the Earth, a dewdrop on the tip of a leaf, the ultimate, profound, amazing truth is everywhere, indwelling yet all-pervasive, personal yet unlimited.

If you follow our suggestions in previous chapters for entering into direct experience of the heart, you will come naturally to moments of luminous awareness as part of the flow of your experience. This chapter is about recognizing and clarifying luminous awareness and focusing on returning to and remaining within its embrace. This recognizing and remaining is part of the path of the heart essence, an ancient path which arose out of direct experience in the wilderness long before it was known as Mahasandhi, Maha Ati, Dzogchen, or The Great Perfection. The complete path of the heart essence is the union of luminous awareness and the visions of inner radiance. Tögal is the practice of this union, and the path is incomplete without Tögal, yet without recognition of luminous awareness as an engaged openness of heart, the visions will not unfold in a genuine way. The same essence manifesting as the visions of inner radiance also manifests as the natural world, and if our hearts are open and our minds are allowing, we can enter the flow of luminous awareness through the radiance that is here all around us as the vision that is this life.

THE FOUR RECOGNITIONS

There are four guiding recognitions of the path of the heart essence: openness, transcendence, spontaneous presence, and oneness. They are each facets of luminous awareness and are traditionally meant to guide you to deepening experience of the blended openness that is in your heart and in the natural world. You may have already touched them through some of the practices we have suggested earlier, or they may have arisen naturally for you in the course of your life. Like the four qualities of the Earth, they are aspects of a seamless whole, which you experience decisively as you reach fruition in the practice of Tögal, but you begin to touch all four qualities within this manifest world. They are reflections of the intent of essence, intrinsic to our experience of this world, and they are within you right now. People originally lived within the flow of these aspects without needing to differentiate them before the split between mind and heart. Now they are an aid to help your mind recognize and appreciate the widening scope of your heart's perceptions and the depth of aware experience available to you.

Awareness is natural, it is not esoteric; it is the birthright of all beings, sounding from the stars, the whisper of a leaf, the rippling voice of a mountain stream, the vibrations of color in the arch of a rainbow. Emphasis on clearing the perceptions of the mind is not enough. After recognizing the four qualities, you need to begin interacting with the radiance manifesting as this world directly in your own experience through luminous awareness. You need to look through its eyes.

OPENNESS

If you live with the Earth, you will naturally come to experience the quality of openness as it is expressed directly by the essence. Openness is right here all around you. It helps you experience what is becoming evident within your heart. Openness is seen in the vast blue sky. Openness is the sky. When you can recognize this quality in a heartfelt, intuitive way, you become aware that it remains, it abides. Watch the sky, it will guide you, it will teach you this expression of the essence. The sky, blue, expansive, and vast, can have clouds forming, moist and billowing, or heavy fog, enveloping and dense, or rain, or snow, but the sky remains, and you know this in your heart. This is the luminous sphere of awareness. Emotions or habits of mind will arise and yet you know the sky of your heart remains, it abides, and in this recognition the emotions or whatever will fade, will seem less real, less significant. By recognizing and remaining, abiding and allowing, the clouds begin to part and slowly fade away.

TRANSCENDENCE

As you recognize the sky-like quality of openness, you also feel a tone within your heart that has no true name or character to pinpoint. This sense or feeling, ineffable, aware, is the space of your heart and the space of everything, beyond the you looking at the sky, beyond sky, undefined, with a knowing outside of concept, a depth of experience. It is like descending into a cave far, far below the surface of the Earth, and in a vast cavern you turn off the lights and rest within absolute darkness, absolute depth. You are standing within the depth of your heart, knowing without knowing; in the same way, transcendence is a tone of manifest essence beyond explanation or description.

SPONTANEOUS PRESENCE

All manifest form is an expression of spontaneous presence, the energy of how things arise. You only need to wait for the dawn on a clear dark night, witnessing the world coming alive in light and color moment by moment, to experience a taste of spontaneous presence, the ephemeral yet ceaselessly arising nature of all phenomena. In Tögal practice, you meet this expressive power of the essence on its own terms. No longer shaped through the lens of ordinary perceptions, the pure primordial delight of manifesting appears as shimmering transparent fluid colors, lines, and forms, and you begin to experience the radiance of the essence free of the limiting avenues of time and space, free of concepts and mind.

The natural world arises in the same way as the visions of Tögal and for the same purpose, so that all beings may return to essence, and the ground, the most fundamental aspect of spiritual practice is to blend with this spontaneously arising intent all around us in nature. This quality of spontaneous presence is why we call nature the vision that is this life. The natural world unfolds in a fluid wash moment by moment and comes alive for you if your heart is open and you blend with its movement, its flow. Watch the sky, the waters, the forests, feel their arising force within you and you will know spontaneous presence within your own life.

When you come to recognize luminous awareness and know spontaneous presence as a friend, an integral aspect of the vision that is this life, then there is no cutting through, as recognition of luminous awareness is sometimes called. Cutting through solidity is a process of the mind, a mind that does not allow the heart to open and does not acknowledge nature as a reflection of the intent of essence. And so that mind is confined to an experience of awareness based solely on words and concepts, ritual games that only allude to freedom.

When one practices in the wholeness, recognizing luminous awareness from the heart, there is no cutting through, only a blended acknowledgment. Then practice is a joy and a fulfillment, a blending with all that manifests moment by moment, spontaneously.

Transcendence and openness are doorways, key recognitions to allow the mind to recognize and accept dimensions of experience outside its more limited areas of expertise. Openness allows the mind to accept, respect, and listen to the energies of the heart. Transcendence helps the mind let go of holding to fixed patterns, to requiring all experience to be reducible to something it can handle on its own terms. But neither openness nor the ineffability of transcendence are sufficient introduction to the wholeness of the path. The mind, no matter how free it perceives its view to be, is still working within its own codes, its own limitations; it is the ability of the heart to embrace experience in a much more dynamic, fluid, feeling way that gives true access to the wholeness at the core of all experience. That is why we have emphasized the heart in all our writings and teachings. Not everyone will do Tögal in this life, but everyone is born with the capacity to live from the heart, to touch and be touched by the essence shining throughout all experience, all manifestation.

Luminous awareness is not an operation of the mind, a higher consciousness to which you ascend. Luminous awareness is direct perception of and by the heart of the aware fluid arising nature of the essence woven throughout all manifestation. It is simply an acknowledgement from your heart of the heart of all. It is around you and within you now. It is snowfall at twilight, a summer breeze, the wings of a butterfly, a rainbow in a misty sky, a small weed in the crack of a sidewalk. It is your wonder at the almost inexpressible beauty and tenderness woven throughout all being.

ONENESS

In the path of Tögal, the four qualities come together as one. Tögal is the path of union, wholeness, the release of all manifestation from separation through direct experience of the spontaneously arising nature of anything and everything as a single seamless expression of the essence.

There are many levels or degrees of the experience of oneness, from the oneness as you open your heart to encompass the hopes and fears of all beings, to the oneness of pure essence. You may have already touched an aspect of oneness while waiting for animals, witnessing the interrelated concentric rings of being, and later as your practice deepened, you may have felt that all myriad manifestation also moves within your heart. There is an even deeper and inconceivably comprehensive level of oneness that you come to in Tögal. As you approach resolution on the path of Tögal, oneness dawns beyond time or space, within a purity of light at the very edge of essence until the moment when all phenomena resolve and only essence remains, a knowing beyond knowing, absolute potential, absolute intent, the seamless single depth of oneness.

Oneness is woven throughout the vision that is this life, and when you enter the natural world with an open heart, you will come to experience a blended bonded feeling that is inexpressible. This is not the same as the final oneness in the path of Tögal; it is a touch, a taste, a glimpse expressed within the sphere of this life, like the barest brilliance of morning light through the trees. As you continue to live and blend with nature, you will feel in your heart an all-encompassing tone, not just looking at sky, but also feeling it seamlessly within your heart. All aspects of the cycle of spiritual growth are found at all levels; you will not have a complete experience of oneness until the embrace, though you need to experience this quality of blended acknowledgement of the heart all along the path. It is a guiding force, the intent of essence speaking to you through the visionary experience that is life.

Oneness is the signature of the spiritual path, the circle through which you are moving home, and at the same time, home itself at every step along the way. You are never apart from the natural intrinsic wholeness of all manifestation. You have never been apart from essence, you are already home; there have never been any divisions. The path of return is the path of deeply experiencing this underlying oneness that is already around you and within you right now, but you come to degrees of this experience gradually. An expression of the all-inclusive oneness already in your life is the web of living energies sometime known as Indra's net.

This luminous web of intent, a reflection of the living continuum of the essence that arises so vividly within the Tögal visions of inner radiance, can be experienced directly within the vision that is this life through opening your heart to another in genuine compassion and love. The jewels at the crossroads of the net can be holy beings, friends, mountains, plants, waters, rivers, oceans, a dewdrop, the light on a windowsill. The essential aspect of Indra's net is the luminous heart to heart connection with all life, the recognition of the primordial essence in all. Every aspect of our daily life is already an integral part of this sacred net of great compassion. Our choice is to open to it and bond with this great union.

Feeling oneness in your heart is the most essential way to train, and as your experience of oneness deepens, luminous awareness can open gently, delicately more and more until it blossoms as the fullness of inner radiance, and you take the last path in which all patterns of energy and manifestation become experienced as truly whole.

LUMINOUS AWARENESS

Luminous awareness is experienced within the sphere of the heart, it arises; it is not constructed or visualized, not conjured out of thoughts or words. The experience of luminous awareness can arise clearly and purely when you touch and are touched by the natural world, a living breathing active blessing speaking to your heart, touching your heart with the rainbow brilliance of sunrise through a dewdrop or an ice crystal, a bright hello popping you out of your confined shell. You come to this experience by feeling, not by thinking. Luminous awareness is not a cocky or disengaged denial of the phenomenal world. Luminous awareness is a glow or brilliance in the heart of all life, simple and natural, in which we all can and should abide. This is original heart.

Luminous awareness is not a concept to ascribe to, nor is it a doctrine to be understood and then followed. Luminous awareness abides within all manifestation, yet it must be found and recognized through a calm allowing mind and an open heart. You need not go far to encounter it; everyone has experienced it at some point in their lives. You are born with an open aware heart. Unfortunately, humans have made their minds dominant over their hearts. We are taught from earliest childhood by initiates of our agreed reality to perceive and function in a world mediated almost entirely by the mind. Many people who come to spiritual practice today fall to the prevailing problem of thinking their feelings and their experience, and when they come to the practices of the heart essence many think their experience of luminous awareness as well.

Luminous awareness is completely, utterly natural; it is outside the realm of words and concepts. It is experienced directly within the heart if your mind is allowing your heart to open. This openness can then touch the heart of essence, the aware openness that extends beyond the confines of our being. This is not a conceptualized idea. When you are centered in the heart's experience of luminous awareness, you will be drawn to the natural world because it resonates with this openness. If you find yourself unwilling or resistant to being in direct relationship with nature in its most fundamental expressions, it is a sign that your mind has a hold over your heart, has created its own experience of awareness, and does not want to be challenged. Luminous awareness is the heart and breath of the intent of essence, it pervades all that naturally manifests, a constant tone of experience felt and touched within your heart, expanding beyond self, an expression beyond confinement, a sense of natural freedom.

RETURNING

THE PRACTICE OF LUMINOUS AWARENESS

Luminous awareness can arise spontaneously in the course of your life and practice, but it is very possible to disregard this subtle change at first and pass over and dismiss the experience, for the tendency of the mind is to be caught up in itself and in maintaining a seemingly real sense of separate identity. The luminous aspect of your heart has a larger scope: unbounded, undefined, sky-like, and clear, an openness with no sense of separate self, touching the continuity of the intent of essence within the ephemeral arising nature of your experience. The more you have nurtured the openness of your heart, the more receptive and aware you will be, and you will be spiritually strong enough to stay within the recognition of luminous awareness and return to it when your mind has wandered off and clouded your experience of the heart. It takes time to gain a heart-based confidence in your ability to return to a genuine experience of awareness rather than being caught up in memories or the mind's concepts of it, and it is crucial to be clear about the difference between a fabricated experience and true luminous awareness of your heart.

There are a number of ways to lead the mind to its own openness that perceives and is in harmony with the luminous awareness of the heart. Many of the suggestions we have already made are for setting up circumstances for the mind to surrender to the heart. Some traditions use the mind to convince itself of its own ghostlike nature as an aid to recognizing awareness, but by far the most effective way is to skip over convincing entirely and not indulge the mind's habit of dwelling on itself. Give yourself to your heart outside of words, allow the heart to blossom and bring you to fruition, letting go of ideas and concepts, the possessions of the mind, letting go of comparisons and judgments, the cherished arenas of the mind.

Luminous awareness is your original heart, one with the fabric of all being. A guide can point out the experience of it to you formally, but this experience also arises naturally within this manifest world. There are countless guides. You can get pointing out from the sky, you can get it from a tree, you can get it from a dewdrop on a leaf, from sunlight on a window sill, from all the myriad expressions of the compassionate intent of essence, wordless, nameless, all around us. And over time this radiant hello will arise more often as you rest within a flow of knowing blended and unconfined. You return again and again, not through memory but here now, to direct experience of your original heart.

The practice of returning to luminous awareness is the practice of not doing anything, not purifying the world or making it into emptiness or an illusion, just allowing it to be as it is. This returning is a reflection of the larger cycle of return to essence moving through all experience. You sit in your posture on the ground outside, return to that expansive aware heart and remain in that direct experience until your mind wanders off. When it wanders, do not berate yourself, just return and settle within the luminous awareness of your heart again. Practicing outside with a spacious unobstructed view of the sky can be very helpful in returning, but wherever you are, whatever you are doing, you return again and again. This is the practice. You sit, you stand, you walk, you eat, all the while returning and continuing in luminous awareness. This level of immersion in the practice is best done in long retreat. You need time to settle into the wholeness of the practice, to allow a genuine heart confidence to grow, returning to this awareness over and over. It takes much time and practice to become stable, but first, you need to be able to return to a clear experience of luminous awareness on your own.

It is very important to be able to settle yourself, to be able to go to your heart and return to luminous awareness readily in any situation. All the avenues that we have suggested in the chapter on letting go are valuable supports, sitting on the Earth in wide-angle vision most of all. Returning is not returning to a previous state, to a memory of an experience of awareness or to an idea or concept of awareness, it is returning the pure, fresh experience in the moment now, unclouded by judgments or comparisons. Returning is being immersed in a clear pond of aware presence, feeling the luminous intent of essence reflected in your heart and the heart of all manifestation moving out softly like ripples across the surface of the water.

THREE SKIES

The three skies practice is a simple and beautiful way to merge into an expansive and fluid experience. In this practice, you blend the clear blue outer sky with the spacious inner sky of your subtle energies and the sky of your heart. Sit outdoors with a generous view of the sky, settle yourself facing away from the sun and breathe gently with your mouth slightly open. Concentrating on the out breath, pour your heart out softly through your eyes as you pour your breath into the blue expanse of space, melding the three skies, and then rest in that expanded sphere. You can also do this lying down. Once you have experience with the feeling of the three skies, you can blend them anywhere, even in a small room. Hopefully when you come to a practice like this you have already had years of experience being in wide-angle vision and letting go of habits of perception and identity; you have a lot of experience sitting within your heart and you can recognize luminous awareness arising spontaneously. This is a practice for when your mind is truly allowing and is not going to break into your experience and make it into its own expression.

INNER RADIANCE

Inner radiance is a deeper experience of the natural luminosity of your heart. Inner radiance is the light of the path itself, the intent of the essence reflected in your heart, blossoming, opening beyond thought or description, fluid, molten, luminous joy, evanescent yet palpable, arising as anything and everything, from the shining dewdrop on a leaf in the early morning, to the light of your own heart. Inner radiance is the moon in a clear sky before dawn, the translucent illumined stems and leaves of a young plant, the shining rainbow, and the iridescent body of an emerging cicada. It is a heightened experience of the luminous awareness spreading out of your heart like light across the sky with an innocent joy.

When your practice of returning to luminous awareness truly ripens, inner radiance begins to blossom naturally, expanding, pushing outward, until, like the calyx around the new bud of a flower, the husk of your obscurations, emotions, and habitual tendencies cracks open and allows this glory of inner light to appear, the natural response of a clear and luminous heart. In those moments as inner radiance dawns, it opens like a flower both within your heart and within the world, a glory of oneness, the effulgence of an inner light, open and gentle, receptive to all. Restrictions fall away; only the subtle light of the heart of essence reflected in your heart remains, suffusing and arising out of all that you perceive.

To allow the very essence of being to guide you, you must be able to allow and then surrender completely to the guiding force of this light within your heart, which will lead you to the threshold of the final most absolute doorway.

SURVIVAL OF ORIGINAL HEART

Opening your heart to the heart of all being through direct experience with the natural world is the core of this book. This is the basic premise, the fundamental focus, that nature, our Earth as it naturally arises, is not just a random event stuck in linear expansionist time. The Earth in all its glory arises for a purpose; there is an intent underlying the physical world, and all of us can relate with and learn from this intent. All we have to do is go to our hearts, surrender to the flow within this luminous globe we live upon and enter a world ready to teach and guide us.

Within this book, we offer a number of ways to reconnect with this natural flow of intent, and by entering this flow, you come to experience luminous awareness directly as a natural state, open to all. Just as in the visions of inner radiance, the vision that is this life is here for us to learn, it is not random; it is an arising intent that can be entered and lived with. Luminous awareness is the breath of this living intent and we can find it naturally within our hearts, free from the confines of the mind.

In our books, *Water Drawn Before Sunrise, Luminous Heart of Inner Radiance,* and now *Luminous Heart of the Earth,* we express the simple reality that this heart experience of living upon the Earth is a primordial original vision that we all can access if we come to it with an open heart free of the confines of the mind. The mind may try to assign a word to it, to describe and then define this world. Let go of all the words, let go of the definitions, the prescribed formats of the mind that only tend to limit and constrict. Then this world that can be directly experienced if we come to it with an open heart and an allowing mind can be seen as it is, a fluid visionary experience, a joy as simple and profound as sitting beside a pond watching dewdrops fall into its surface creating rainbow concentric rings in the early morning light. Do not discount what is simple and small; do not limit yourself to the grand and the spectacular. The simple daily wonders can be the source of the most pivotal lessons, the most extraordinary visions of our lives.

Our world vision we call Earth can be lived with in simplicity within the wonder and living glory that naturally arises. You can still learn how to do this, the techniques are few, but the most important is an open heart. Knowing how to live with our Earth is crucial to shed the basis of fear, the underlying nervousness of contemporary culture. To know in your heart that wherever you are you can live, build a shelter, find water, build a fire, and find food, liberates you from the terrible curse of modern man, the fear of not being home, the fear of being lost, the fear of being helpless. We are here to live simply within this vision of the natural world and follow the personal signs and messages in a heart to heart union with the divine, a spiritual life played out through countless lives embraced by this flow of intent.

But here we are now on an endangered planet. Many species are passing away; the great diversity of natural life is vanishing due to our actions. The ignorance of man is cresting, soon to turn inward and crash down upon itself, an unfortunate reflection of a natural cycle ending this time in a tragic decline. This is almost too bleak to comprehend, yet this is also a time of setting seed, a time of turning inward toward origin, toward what is essential. This is a time to set the seed of your spiritual journey, to concentrate and focus your life, your intent, and all your love into a form that can engender new life. You can embrace this time and change within it, or you can hold to what is collapsing and deny the reality of our situation or try to wish it away.

During times of decline and dissolution there is a gap, an opening where you can choose, shift your perspective, and change. Within this gap, this extraordinary space in time, you can set the seed of new aspects of your path by embracing this gap and changing within it.

Setting seed requires that you look with open eyes to perceive this world from your heart, open like the sky, and with an unclouded view you will know what to do with this gap, this opening within the collapse. Setting seed and an open heart are intertwined with a purpose that all life prospers, experiencing and learning within the active movement of a generative love. These books are our way of sowing the seeds that we have set, our way of loving; they are our way of calling out into the tumult of our times so others who feel as we do will take on the challenge of living simply within this vision, moving into a time when this generative love will again grow and flourish.

While we lived in Costa Rica near the tropical highland forest, we saw the power of this generative love within nature and how omnipresent is its expression if left alone to arise and flourish. If you come from an open heart relating with all that naturally manifests, you will experience this love. It is this generative love that will heal the wounds of our world, preparing the ground for another age.

We each have an opportunity and a sacred responsibility now at the time of setting seed to make choices that will engender a future of harmony with the intent of the essence arising naturally all around us. We pray that out of the dissolution of this age will come another age when the natural world will be seen again through the heart, as the heart. There will be no separation, no distinction of other, but a knowing, loving embrace of a sacred vision, like the curving petals of a flower unfolding and radiating outward from the seed, a natural blending of union, fluid like water, expansive like the air, brilliant like the sun.

Artists Robert and Rachel Olds spent nine years in retreat together integrating Earth living and the practices of the heart essence of Dzogchen. They came to their retreat after years of spiritual inquiry through their artwork and years of letting go and simplifying their lives to connect more fully with the natural world. They share the unique perspective that their completion of the path of Tögal brings to encourage recognition that this Earth, this vision we call life, is a sacred offering.

They offer teachings of direct experience within the natural world for opening to the luminous awareness in your heart and embracing the radiant expression we call life. Their other books include *Luminous Heart of Inner Radiance* and *Water Drawn Before Sunrise*.

www.acircleisdrawn.org

Made in the USA
San Bernardino, CA
30 January 2016